"SURVIVAL GUIDE"
to
Law Enforcement
Promotional Preparation
2nd Edition

By

J.L. Redick

JLConsulting Solutions, LLC

"Survival Guide" To Law Enforcement Promotional Preparation
ISBN 978-1-7373694-1-7   Softbound
ISBN 978-1-7373694-2-4   E-Book
Copyright © 2019, 2021. Jonni L. Redick
All rights reserved.
Original published by Amazon, Kindle Direct Publishing 2019.
Second Edition by Curry Brothers Publishing, 2021.

No parts of this publication may be reproduced, stored in a retrieval system, or transmitted in any form or by any means, electronic, mechanical, photocopying, recording, or otherwise, without the prior written permission of the copyright owner.

This book is sold subject to the condition that it shall not, by way of trade or otherwise, be lent, resold, hired out, or otherwise circulated without the publisher's prior consent in any form of binding or cover other than that in which it is published and without a similar condition including this condition being imposed on the subsequent purchaser. Under no circumstances may any part of this book be photocopied for resale.

This is a work of nonfiction; however, to protect privacy, some experiences were blended with fictitious people. Any similarity between the characters and situations within its pages and places or persons, living or dead, is unintentional and co-incidental.

Cover Design by Alex Cotton *(Unrelenting Media).*
Editing by Cheryl and William Greene
Cover Photography by Frederick D. James *(FDJ Photography)*
Infographics by Chanel Curry *(Creative License Consulting)*

Table of Contents

Introduction..iii

Chapter 1. Am I Even Ready? Assessing Your Own Readiness to Promote.............1

Chapter 2. How, Where, When Do I Even Begin?..11

Chapter 3. How to Study for a Written Test: Study Stacking....................................17

Chapter 4. What Do I Do in the Wait between the Written and Oral Panel Interview?..23

Chapter 5. Preparing for the Oral Panel Interview & Assessment Center.............29

Chapter 6. GAME DAY..37

Chapter 7. Results Day..43

Chapter 8. It's All Over - Or is it?..49

ANNEX A. Career Development Planning Template..56

ANNEX B. Example of a 10-Week Promotional Written Examination Study Group Plan..59

ANNEX C. Sample Study Workshop Schedule: Oral Panel Interview....................63

ANNEX D. Sample Study Workshop or Study Plan Schedule Written and Oral Panel Interview..67

ANNEX E. Examples of Mock Interview and Scenario Questions.........................71

ANNEX F. Example Study Checklist Format (EEO) 73

ANNEX G. Assessment Center Overview and Approach..........................77

ANNEX H. Oral Panel Interview and Assessment Center Response Strategy Technique..87

ANNEX I. Sample Prompts Oral Panel Interview Questions and Written Exercise..93

ANNEX J. Practice Exercise - Captain...95

ANNEX K. Sample In-Basket Practice Exercise.....................................97

ANNEX L. Mnemonics (Acronyms) Building Exercise.........................105

ANNEX M. Basic Project Management: Oral Panel Interview and Assessment Center Response Strategies..107

ANNEX N. Mental Thought Mapping Exercise....................................109

About The Author...113

Author Contact Information..115

Introduction

How do you know if you're ready to promote? And why should you? *The "Survival Guide" to Law Enforcement Promotional Preparation* emerged from my own personal experience of navigating why, how, where, and when to even begin the journey of promotion.

Early in my law enforcement career, I had a desire to promote. Having a desire and an actual plan are two vastly different things. Many times, in organizations, when it comes to promoting and preparing for testing, people get very reclusive and not helpful to others. It's like being in a private club, you only get in with a special invitation. Once I was able to learn how to become better prepared for the promotional examinations process, I developed a framework for others that was just as successful. The study sessions were concise, systematic, and effective.

As I was navigating understanding how to study for promotions, I was also learning how to create my own career path and be a leader on the way to them. With a vision of building better 21st Century leaders, it became clear it was not all about organizational transactional metrics in a tactile way, but metrics in transformative behaviors that manifest into authentic, compassionate, and servant leadership. Through my own leadership ascension, the mantle of helping others promote and build their leadership became an imperative. It became my purpose and WHY for writing the *"Survival Guide" to Law Enforcement Promotional Preparation*.

The "Survival Guide" to Law Enforcement Promotional Preparation gives guidance on how to set the cadence of your study plan that is designed by you and self-paced based on your needs. Additionally, there are important reminders on managing your emotions, stress and finding a life balance while navigating promotional processes within your organization. As the exercises and content within the book shape your discipline for preparation, it also creates a foundation of understanding on how to leverage your resources, experience, and network to strengthen your opportunities for overall career success while growing your leadership acumen. It is a resource to share what was always so secretly coveted in those private study groups... knowledge, understanding, championing.

Throughout my own journey, I've discovered a greater purpose in my promotions, and I hope that you will too.

Chapter 1

Am I Even Ready?
Assessing Your Own Readiness to Promote

Why is assessing your own readiness to promote important? That's a great question. I found out early in my career when I first started thinking about promoting, I thought I knew what I didn't really know at all. It took me several years to understand this – I didn't know all that I thought I did. It wasn't until I recognized this undeniable fact that I was able to bring the best me to the promotional process.

There is great value in the research that shows that studying for promotional examinations result in better success rates. How you study and what you study increases not only your success rate, but how you grow your knowledge, sharpen your leadership skills, and have a better perspective of the broader implications in your organization and the industry. Participating in the examination process for promotion is more than passing the test, it's about building better leaders for the 21st Century.

"Evaluating Self"

One of the first areas in my personal assessment is what I call "evaluating self." When I embarked on the promotional roller coaster, I had no idea what I was getting into. While needing to spend the appropriate time studying, I also needed to be mentally and emotionally ready. I honestly just looked around at other people who were taking the tests and told myself, "If they can do it, so can I." Now some might call that having initiative and being bold, and while I will agree with that to some extent, when I look back I realize, I was not emotionally ready or prepared.

The first time I took the sergeant's test, which is the first promotional process after being a sworn officer, I was 25 years old. I had barely any life experience and only been on the job for about 4 years. Some young people are ready, I was NOT. So, the first time I took the test, I thought I didn't need to study and didn't need anyone's help. I failed. The second time I took the test I rationalized to myself that I had really studied hard but in actuality, I hadn't and also, I hadn't had much mentoring either. As a result, I failed again.

Before I get to the next time I took the test, I must remind you that time had passed and I had accumulated another 4 years of life experience, as well as having experienced the birth of my two children and 4 more years of time on the job. Without me really noticing, life was maturing me, growing me in responsibility and accountability. Also, discovering that having a study plan of some kind might be helpful, even one that wasn't that great. "The 3rd time is always the charm," my mother would say. I took the test again. It felt like forever to get the results back. I passed, barely.

At the same time, I was juggling raising a 6-year-old and a 2-year-old while working the graveyard shift. I must have been insane to think I actually wanted to promote! I think my impetus was, I saw those promoting around me, and some of them, well, I didn't see many of them as anything extraordinary, but they were able to make that list and get promoted.

Consider These Questions to Assess Your Emotional Readiness

As I reflect on my first journey through the examination process, I began to recognize the value of knowing one's own emotional readiness before making the decision to test and promote. Emotional readiness is different than emotional intelligence which for me has evolved over the years.

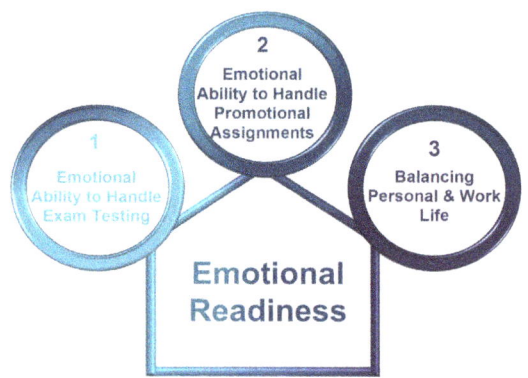

Emotional intelligence is the capacity to be aware of, control and express your emotions. It is also having the ability to manage your emotions in a positive way to communicate more effectively, empathize with others, and defuse conflict. Through the process of understanding and discovering your emotional intelligence quotient, you grow your social awareness and increase your ability to create better outcomes through better decision making and problem solving. When I refer to emotional readiness, I'm talking about the emotional ability to handle the journey of examination testing, promotional assignments and balancing your personal life and your work life.

One of the exercises I have taken myself through, and many of those I've coached, is to take time and physically write your answers to the following questions. Reading them may be helpful, but when you write them down and discuss them with your family, it changes the level of authenticity in your responses. It can be quite an eye-opening experience because while our minds can process thousands of thoughts at a time, when we write something down, it takes our brains much longer to process. As a result, it makes a somewhat indelible impression on our consciousness.

Here are some questions to ask yourself as you assess your own readiness:

- What is your "why" for wanting to promote?

- Do you have the right attitude for the responsibility of the position? When you promote, you take those beginning steps towards leadership, and you need to be sure that you are in a position to model the proper leadership behavior to others. You must have made that behavior a part of your personality and be demonstrating it on a daily basis in your current role. If you're not, check yourself and begin to correct that behavior.

- Is making more money your catalyst? Money should not be the only reason to seek a leadership position; truthfully, it should never be the reason to promote and if that is your only motivation, you will be setting yourself up for a bumpy journey.

- Are you emotionally ready for the time, energy, stress, expectations, and commitment you will need to put forth to prepare and take the test?

- Have you talked to your support system and how do they feel? Do they know what it will take for the examination, for the promotion?

- Does your spouse understand, will your spouse resent you, or feel like they are competing with you? How do you talk through this ahead of time?

- Are you willing to sacrifice and compromise your personal life for your professional life to test and promote?

- Are you willing to be vulnerable as emotions will run high and others will challenge your competency?

- Are you ready to compete? (Mostly against yourself, but it is a competition).

- Are you strong enough to fail? Will you persevere and try again? Remember, this is only to take the test, promoting is an entirely different level of readiness but you must have the foundation to start the journey.

- How do you define your own readiness? Did you check with anyone else, mentors, or leadership in the organization?

- Are you afraid of succeeding? I realize it's a strange question to ask, but it is a reality that sometimes we fear the very thing we are seeking the most.

- Do you have a good balance of things to enrich your spirit, your mental and physical health, and your overall wellness? Overall wellness will be important as to how well you will endure the experience of the promotional processes and the actual promotion itself.

Assessing Your Tangible Work Experience

After you have spent some time in self-reflection assessing your emotional readiness, the next step is to assess your tangible work experience that will be needed to support your competency and prepare you for the examination and the promotion.

For example, I really didn't understand that just doing a good job as a road officer may not be enough for what I wanted to be – a field sergeant. In other words, to just do your job or even do it well may not be enough when it comes to promotion. Promotion involves taking on additional tasks and responsibilities and as a result, we need to start being more than one who simply meets the daily minimum requirement. Mediocrity should not be an acceptable form of performance and certainly does not demonstrate the true leadership skills necessary when you decide to promote.

Personally, I had tunnel vision - not knowing what I didn't need to know kept my job easy and comfortable. I didn't understand that I needed to think about how I could either get involved in bigger projects, handle more responsibility, and sometimes, yep, even sometimes volunteer my time towards things for which I may not get paid. Trust me, I just didn't get it. I had always felt that doing my job as a patrol officer was both stressful and fun; but, in itself, more than enough. When you add in the struggles of my personal life - juggling being a young mother and wife of another police officer and commuting long distances so we could afford to buy a home, it was a tough balance. Thankfully, over time, I learned the importance of planning along with finding good mentors to give me advice. We'll talk more about mentors, coaches and sponsors later.

So how do you assess this part of your personal readiness when you feel like what you're doing already should be enough, or if you feel you have way too much on your plate? Here are a few questions and suggestions to ponder as you continue to engage in honest self-reflection and assessment.

- When is the last time you sat down and listed all the awesome things you've done professionally or personally? Physically writing down all of your accomplishments helps to build your confidence and creates a list of experiences that will hopefully correlate with the promotion that you are seeking.

- Where are your blind spots in your work and volunteer inventory?

- Remember that the prior life and work experience you bring with you into an organization is valuable. It is important to determine how that experience may correlate with the position that you are seeking.

- If you volunteer in nonprofit work, do you supervise, plan, coordinate, handle budgets, or collaborate on projects? Consider all of your experiences, knowledge, and skills that may apply to the promotional position.

- If you want to contribute more to the organization, what would you want to do? What does the organization need that you could provide with your skills, knowledge, and experience?

- In order to take advantage of the advancement opportunities that you are seeking, be very strategic on how you will need to grow your experience, knowledge, skills, and abilities. Try to determine what will best build your competency and make you a more well-rounded candidate.

- Are you a continual learner? When was the last time you took any training that wasn't mandated? College or adult learning classes?

The Importance of Mentors, Coaches & Sponsors

Another part of the assessment process is to make sure you identify and acquire good mentors, coaches and sponsors that can guide you through all stages of your journey.

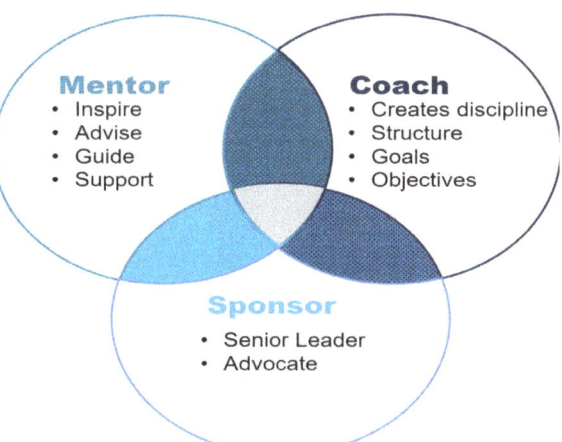

Mentors and coaches both want to see you succeed; however, the difference in a mentor and a coach are very different. Mentors will inspire, advise, guide, and help you whenever and wherever they can and are extremely important to success in your journey. Coaches will create discipline, structure, goals, and objectives for you so that you can reach your desired outcomes. Coaches can improve your ability to focus, drive your momentum and build your acumen in those areas that you will need in order to be successful. Having one or both of them will greatly increase your opportunities for success in your career goals and provide the leverage to optimize your leadership journey.

When I was a young inexperienced officer in my twenties, I had a mentor that was not necessarily the same type of mentor I would need as an experienced captain in my forties. In fact, as I rose through the ranks, I realized that I needed more than a mentor. I needed a coach who could provide me consistency and structure. Investing in me was the best thing I could have ever done. I just wish it had occurred to me sooner.

Each mentor and coach should bring something to your toolbox that you can't provide for yourself. They should be experienced, well rounded in their own personal and professional development, and be able to have real-talk with you about all that's good and all that's not so good. I will tell you, this isn't easy when it's not so good - our pride can get hurt very quickly. However, if you can take it as constructive criticism given to you so that you might become a better leader and if you can learn from it and not take it personally, you will find, in most instances, it's really about developing you and making you all that you can be.

One suggestion about identifying mentors specifically, they won't necessarily reach out to you. Often, you will need to be bold enough to go out and seek your mentors and ask them to work with you. I remember very specifically asking a male executive leader if he would be my mentor. He was a little taken aback and didn't really have a response other than, "Sure, I guess so." I wasn't offended that it was a lackluster response. I suppose it's possible he wasn't expecting that request from a female subordinate that didn't work directly in his chain of command. But I'd discovered the only way I was going to leverage my opportunities to grow my career network, knowledge and have exposure to the space I was striving to reach was to obtain a mentor I trusted within that realm. That realm was where I wanted to get to, and I needed someone who was already there and was willing to help me work on what I needed to reach my destination. He ended up being an even better sponsor and his initial reaction was not because he was lackluster, it was because no woman had ever asked him to be her mentor.

Seeking out a mentor can be a bit awkward initially. However, if you're both professional and invested in having a meaningful interaction and positive experience, mentorship can be an amazingly effective tool.

Here are some things my mentors and coaches helped me to assess for my readiness to promote:

- "Why do you want to promote?" Remember, in the early assessment, your WHY is always going to be important.

- Do you know what's required of the position? If you don't, it's highly recommended that you do your research. You can find expectations and performance evaluation criteria for the positions usually in your manual, or on a monthly or annual evaluation form.

- Do you have a career development plan? If you don't have one, have someone show you an example of one or check with your Human Resources department. (See Annex A of this guide).

- What are your short-term and long-term career goals? Do they align with your personal values? Why does this matter? It matters because if your personal values are not in alignment with your career goals as you embark on your promotional journey you will need to assess your emotional readiness.

- Am I ready for the additional challenges and stress associated with the next level of promotion?

- What have you contributed above and beyond the basic job duties of the position you're in now?

- Have you started looking at additional training opportunities or additional special assignments?

- Have you been engaging in the community both at work and personally?

- Have you found ways to be more visible to those in leadership while getting exposure to the position that you are seeking? How does this help to demonstrate your readiness for the promotion?

- Are you a continual learner? What requirements do some of your career goals have that may require you to have more training, more education, and a more global understanding of issues?

- Do you have a strong discipline regarding reading? Over the years reading in general and especially reading books has improved my IQ tremendously. In many areas it has created in me a greater overall understanding of the world and helped me to build a depth of correlated information that has significantly improved my creative, communication, and leadership skills. Thus, significantly helping to expand my sphere of influence.

- Are you going to apply for that promotion even if you don't think you meet all the requirements? Rest assured some will compete even without all the requirements. Others will often wait until they have all the requirements, something close to perfection, before entering the competition. For a number of us women, we wait on getting it all perfect, or close to it, before we will put in for a position, or even interview for the opportunity. Why wait, just do it!

Finally, having a sponsor can be a key factor in your career success. There are several similarities to a mentor, or even a coach, but a sponsor is often a senior leader in an organization and advocates for you in rooms you don't have the opportunity to be in yet. Good trustworthy and reliable sponsors are difficult to obtain because they could be inundated with solicitations and may not have the bandwidth to keep everyone at the forefront. One way to gain a sponsor, and get their attention, is to earn it. Make sure you are doing your work with excellence, not perfection, simply good solid work.

Always focus on building your skills in those important leadership competencies: emotional intelligence, decisiveness, sound judgment, inclusiveness, interpersonal skills, change management and other skills. Then remember to let your leadership know your career aspirations and about the projects you're working on. Market yourself, without being overbearing, but with confidence, it is okay. Sponsors are incredibly valuable and can create exponential opportunities for you.

Now that you have put yourself through a self-assessment of your own readiness, it's time to figure out where to start the journey!

Chapter 2

How, Where, When Do I Even Begin?

If you thought that assessing your readiness for promotion was a vulnerable process, it was only the beginning of what you will need to begin doing to be ready. This chapter will provide you with an example of how to begin to prepare for the actual examination process.

Understanding an Examination Cycle

First things first, you should understand your agency's examination cycle. By knowing when the next examination will occur, you will be able to determine if you're eligible to even participate in the process. Also knowing the timing of the exam helps you in planning for when and how to prepare. Some promotional eligibility lists can be 12 months, 24 months, or as long as 5 years in length, or in some instances, for a period of time determined by your human resources department often in concurrence with your department head. Having full and complete knowledge of these time frames allows you to plan your preparation accordingly.

Studying for a promotional exam can seem endless, so having an end in sight is helpful. Why? Well, for example, let's say you're ready to promote but the exam is 2 years away, how do you plan for that? When do you start studying? Unfortunately, there are many who don't understand the machinery of the examination cycles let alone the process. It gives you an advantage to learn the underpinning of the HR processes and how that affects you for preparation.

If the examination process timing is unknown, ASK someone! More than likely, you will want to ask your HR department. It should not be a secret and they will have an estimate based on the expiration of the current list on when the next examination might take place.

Here are a few things to consider as a foundational approach after you've vetted the examination cycle frequency:

- Have you reviewed the examination bulletin or announcement? You know that document with all the words in the small font. It is actually very useful. Make sure you read and understand the bulletin details and that you meet all the requirements in it before you apply for the exam.

- Is there an application that must be submitted? If so, you should work on drafting it sooner than later so you don't have to stress over it and be distracted from the actual study regimen you'll be starting. Make sure to have someone in a higher position review your application to make sure you are providing the right kind of information.

Generally in city, county, and state government this form is to qualify you for participation in the exam though other agencies may review it for additional purposes including scoring. I would check with your HR department to gain an understanding of its purpose so you know how much work you need to put into it. If this is your second time taking an examination, then dust off the last one, update it and have it ready early.

It is your responsibility to make sure your application gets to your HR department, so either hand-deliver it or get a secured delivery before the post mark date in the bulletin or announcement. Again, make sure to go over the scope of the bulletin and adhere to all the details and dates within it.

- What requirements are there for submission to participate in the examination beyond the application? Is there a fee? What forms are needed? Is there an Education and Experience (E&E) required? What are the timeframes? Where do you process or send the information?

- Go through the scope of the bulletin and identify the policy manuals and materials you will need to study for the examination based on the stated knowledge and skills required. Is the required reading? Do you have access for all the required materials to study from your agency?

- For some agencies, you'll need to begin to identify new policy information that is not included in permanent policy, but is located in publications such as agency directives, management memorandums, bulletins, information contained on the organization's website, and/or part of the agency head's vision statement. All of which may be included in the examination process.

Other agencies will provide candidates with exactly what is needed to study including additional required reading which will all be available through HR and include a study guide document.

Seek out internal information from the subject matter experts (SME) or HR within your agency to help narrow your focus on what will be applicable to study for your examination. The SMEs or offices of primary interest (OPI) may even have study packets available to applicants for their areas of primary interest.

- Review any recent executive/command management staff meeting minutes to identify contemporary focus topics.

- Make time to meet with those who have already taken the examination you are preparing for and ask if they will share how they prepared for it. (There is an element of confidentiality about the content of an exam, but it does not mean you shouldn't reach out for the pieces of the process they can share with you to help you familiarize yourself with it).

While there is no precise time on when you should start studying, if you're not actively preparing to study well ahead of the actual examination, then you will be behind the curve. I know this because the first time I took an examination, and ok, the second time as well, I had no clue as to study time frames and I took it all for granted. As you read in Chapter 1, I failed a couple of times. So, it would behoove you to get prepared well before an examination announcement is posted so you don't have to feel stressed or pressured at the last minute.

Wait, do you even know what an examination bulletin is or looks like? Just thought of that as I wrote it. I really don't want to assume you know, and I apologize if you do, but to make sure you're fully prepared, I'll explain it anyway.

Job and Examination Bulletins

Job and examination bulletins can be found through your HR department, either internally on your own agency intranet, or externally through the HR website. If you have trouble finding them, ask your supervisor, manager, or HR specialist for one. I find these very helpful in preparing for any examination. An examination bulletin, notice, or flyer provides much of the following:

1. Job Description

2. Duty Statement

3. Promotional assignment

4. Position Details
   a. Working Title
   b. Classification
   c. Salary

5. Minimum Requirements
   a. Who may apply
   b. Understanding the class specifications

6. Special Requirements

7. Application Instructions
   a. How to apply
   b. Where to mail in the application

8. Desirable Qualifications
   a. For example, there is a benefit in knowing that in addition to your abilities based on your own experience you may be further evaluated based on other qualifications as well.
      - Ability to be tactful and maintain a good rapport with departmental employees, peers, supervisors, and the public.
      - Good organizational skills and attention to detail.
      - Ability to multi-task and meet a monthly cut off time frame.

- Ability to work independently on tasks while maintaining the team environment.

9. Required application documents needed
    a. Supplemental questionnaire
    b. Resume

10. Description of the examination process

11. Examination dates for each phase

12. Location of examination

13. Contact information

14. Establishment of the list and how long the list will last

Do not underestimate the value of the actual job posting or examination bulletin for the position or examination. It has a lot of information that you'll want to be aware of moving forward. Keep it with your study or interview preparation material so you can refer to it as needed.

Remember, there is no exact science as to when your preparation should begin. It's really a matter of getting prepared. So, as we close out this chapter, I would strongly emphasize you make sure to thoroughly review your assessment of readiness from Chapter 1 & 2 to make sure the building blocks from your background, experience and preparation are in order and are ready to provide the solid foundation for your plan of study.

Chapter 3

How to Study for a Written Test: Study Stacking

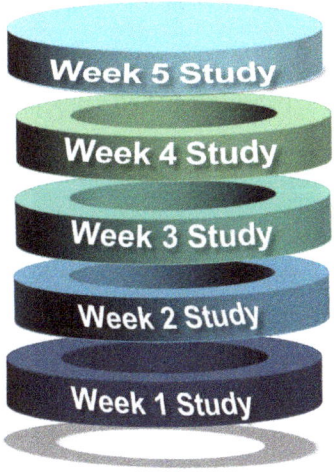

Well, you've survived and made it to Chapter 3. The first two chapters can be overwhelming as you have to stop and really do some self-reflection and a lot of homework as you lay the foundation for moving forward. I know that for myself, when I stopped to think about the totality of what I was embarking on, it made me pause and ask myself if what I was attempting to do was actually worth it. I can tell you, after 29 years of law enforcement, and a 22-year journey of examination processes for various promotions, it was more than worth it. I have had the privilege and opportunity to help so many others reach their goals and that is such a rewarding feeling.

This chapter will help you navigate a study plan for the written examination that will minimize the feeling of being overwhelmed by all of the information you've collected. Before I jump into how to set up your plan, I encourage you, if possible, to find an appropriate study group. Better yet, seek out a study group being led by someone who is in a higher position as they have been where you are now and are, in most cases, where you want to be. I will also share a promotional study group workshop example in Annex B.

Stacking Your Study Plan

Many individuals while studying for promotion use a concept called stacking. So, what is stacking? Basically, stacking is a process of simply placing something on top of something else. It sounds simple enough, but when studying large volumes of information, it can help give a systematic structure to the process that will help decrease that feeling of being overwhelmed and reinforce the learning experience. The process of stacking will give you a way of consistently creating self-discipline for each week's study. Each week when you complete the assignments you will stack that week's work onto the next week's assignments and review. You repeat this process throughout the study schedule that you have previously planned.

This is an example of a 10-week stacking study plan. Before you start, plan how much time you will need to allocate each week to individual study or to the study group. Preferably, you should meet with the study group one day a week. You want to make sure you also have individual study time as everyone studies differently. However, if you are studying on your own and not joining a study group, you really need to have the discipline to stay on your schedule that you've designated for study.

Things to consider for your study plan:
- Highlight and prioritize the agency policy manuals, legal statutes, legislation, compliance regulations and compliance policy, required book reading, and other materials you will want to study first or group together. Are you studying for sergeant, lieutenant, captain or above? This will shift the emphasis of where in each policy manual or general order you will spend more time studying. You can get a list of your agency policy from your publications unit or HR department.

When reviewing policy material, for example, ask yourself as you go through policy, "What shall the sergeant, lieutenant, or captain know?" "What shall the lieutenant know?" Yes, I snuck in a SHALL. Questions will be specifically from policy so know SHOULD and MAY from SHALL. Details will matter and knowledge of your current position and the one you are testing for will be your focus. When you move up in leadership, you should be competent in your current role because you will be responsible for knowing what your subordinates are required to do.

How to Study for a Written Test

Most exams will have a balance of field and administrative policy. As you move up in rank, you will be responsible for knowing more about administrative regulatory and compliance policies on a larger scale for the organization on top of what you are already should know from your officer or supervisory ranks.

- Identify those policy manuals, articles, books or materials that may have peripheral information that you will need to have some knowledge of but may not be essential. However, you never know what may be on a test. So, prioritize these materials as well.

- Create a schedule for your study time that is reasonable. I recommend at least 3-5 days a week for 1-2 hours. Anything too short is worthless and anything too long is exhausting. You could break up the amount of time you plan to study in to smaller segments of time and create micro learning sessions.

- Develop methods that will insure your retention of information. Are you an audio, visual, kinesthetic, or multi-sensory learner? Knowing this will help you decide if you need to create flash cards, voice recordings, video, or sit and have someone verbally go over the material with you, or if some form of all these will help you retain your information better.

- Understand that the amount of studying you do will be different if the exam is a long way off as opposed to when the exam gets closer.

- Stick to your Plan!

Sample Study Stacking Plan Schedule

10-week study plan: 1 session a week for the written test if in a study group. (Example is for a police sergeant/lieutenant examination).

Note: Materials to study should include general orders, management memorandums, policy manuals or directives, laws and codes, and material relevant to the position. It is your responsibility to ensure all materials are current and updated.

Week 1: Create your study session calendar with all the policies you will study week by week at the beginning. With some law enforcement agencies, there are hundreds of policies, procedures, laws and content to filter through. Since you've already prioritized your material, select 2-3 policy manuals or segments to review each week.

Review the material with the idea of looking for what you will need to know to qualify for the position for which you are testing. If the test is for sergeant, what does a sergeant need to know? If it's for lieutenant, what does a lieutenant need to know? If it's for any position, what do YOU need to know for that position? This will help you scan information versus reading every word and focus on the information that is relevant for your study.

You can create outlines of the material that you're studying, but I also recommend creating 20-25 questions and answers from each piece of material you have selected to study. Place this information in several places based on how you identified your learning style from above. The questions will be used in different ways which I'll explain.

The questions from this week's study can be used to create a weekly quiz to test your knowledge and retention. You will also retain the questions and accumulate them into a larger mid-term test of your knowledge and a final exam test of your knowledge at the end of the 10 weeks. You can also find quizzing apps that allow you to create your own quiz questions that might be helpful in that format as well.

Week 2: Take the quiz from Week 1 first. Grade your quiz and only keep the right answers. Get rid of all of the wrong answers. Review your Week 1 outlines, notes, flashcards, etc. Then begin studying your next 2-3 manuals and materials you've identified from your study schedule. Repeat the Week 1 process by outlining and creating 20-25 quiz questions and answers.

Create your quiz.

Repeat this process each week until week 5.

Week 5: Mid-term exam. Start your session with administering yourself a mid-term exam from the first five weeks of quiz questions and answers. Limit yourself to about 50-75 questions so you don't get overwhelmed. Score the exam and keep only the right answers. Answers are verbatim from policy. Continue with your study session schedule.

Repeat this process each week until week 9.

Week 9: Administer a final exam to yourself from a selection of all of the correct quiz questions you have banked over the last 9 weeks. Score this exam and only keep the correct answers. The exam should be approximately 110 questions or the number you'd be taking in a real examination. Provide yourself with the same allotted time you'd receive in a real testing environment, if possible.

All of your materials should have been reviewed, discussed or quizzed on by week 9. You can take all of your notes, correct answers from quizzes, key elements from policies, or other material and create a final preparation document that will reduce all of your study material into one 40-75 page document for study. The length of your final study document will be based on how much material you put together initially.

Note: Remember, get rid of ALL WRONG ANSWERS. Only keep CORRECT ANSWERS. You may carry around a large binder through most of the process until these final weeks. When you get down to the last couple of weeks, your materials should be comprised of only this final study document.

Week 10: Go over your final study document repeatedly for most of the week. Try to relax the day before the exam. On the morning of the exam, be sure to hydrate, relax and just go take the test. If you stay disciplined and follow the process, the answers will literally jump off the page.

See ANNEX RESOURCES for additional details and examples.

Chapter 4

What Do I Do in the Wait Between the Written and Oral Panel Interview?

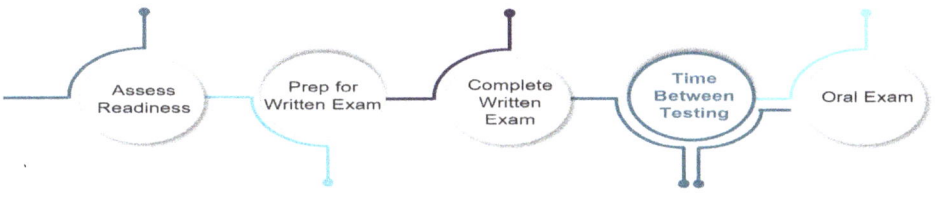

Are you still with me? After all that, you may have decided to put this book down and take a nap. So, at this point, you have successfully finished assessing your readiness, preparing for the written exam, and actually taken the written exam. Are you done yet? Nope. There's more! Let's look at what you might want to do in between the phases of your testing process.

Some examination processes have various components that may include:

- Resumes - sometimes beforehand with the application or sometimes during the process.
- Some form of an oral panel interview or an assessment center process. I will explain more in Chapter 5.
- A written assignment requested in between the written and oral panel interview components. However, you may have just a written test or just an oral panel interview only.

Resumes

What if a resume is required? Do you have one? If you have never prepared a resume, get started putting one together. You might want to research examples of resumes on the internet; seek guidance from a leader in your agency; ask for help from someone who has gone through the process before; or check with one of your mentors or coaches. Make sure that you follow any organizational rules or guidelines for preparing the resume such as certain formatting specifications, number of pages and/or specific information that may be requested.

Important aspects of resumes may not only include formatting, but content. Make sure to be very descriptive in how you articulate your work assignments, duties, skills, experience, and education. Often within a job bulletin or specification, there are words and phrases that can be used to help you craft your own verbiage that will best describe your experience and qualifications suitable for the position.

NOTE: Resumes required in an examination process will be designed much differently than those required for positions outside of an examination process. Be prepared to revamp your resume after an examination so it might be better suited for submission on internal assignments and any external opportunities. Resumes are scored in many examination processes and will impact your final score.

What your resume should contain:
- Job Title
- Experience
- Professional Development: Education, Specialized Assignments, Training
- Certifications
- Professional and Community Organizations
- Significant Committees/Projects

When crafting your resume, focus on your assignments, work experience, community engagement and education. Be certain to remove any fluff or laudatory and inconsequential material. The resume is needed for the assessors to use in your examination process so they can better evaluate your readiness for promotion based on the diversity and breadth of your work experience and education. As you prepare your resume, it is a good idea to review and identify areas you may want to strengthen as you continue in your career.

Remember, the most current information you place in a resume is the most impactful. However, if you had an important and dynamic work assignment a bit earlier in your career, glean what is relevant from that experience, correlate it to the position that you're testing for and include it in the resume. Don't forget that you can include other experience from other employment, work in your community, or other areas of life experience. Any and all information that might demonstrate your knowledge, ability, and overall suitability for the promotion should be included.

Try to incorporate descriptive language that will accurately convey your duties or activities versus just using departmental lingo or simply putting an assignment down without fully explaining what skills were needed. Be clear and concise while painting a picture for the reviewer. Don't make them guess about what you might have had to do in a particular position or assignment.

Always keep your resume current. One final note on resumes, they should not be a novel in length. Usually, they are only one to two pages. They're a snapshot of your work life and history. Make sure to read your instructions and FOLLOW THEM!

Written Assignments

Is there a written assignment to be included in the process? Have you ever completed a written assignment for an examination process? Some examinations will require you to respond to prompts or questions. They are usually two or three-part questions in written form that are often submitted prior to your in-person oral panel interview or assessment center. The intent of this exercise is to see how you process information, create strategy in your approach, and problem solve through the question. Additionally, how you communicate the correlation of your response to your knowledge of organizational policy, procedures, compliance statutes and legal requirements.

There will also be very specific instructions on formatting and limitations on the length of the response to those questions. For example, when I took the captain's examination, I had to respond to three prompts that were very multi-layered and complex on ONE page. I had always felt that I was a relatively natural communicator both verbally and in written form, but I had no idea how I was going to achieve that requirement.

What I figured out over time was that while I was practicing and preparing the responses, I shouldn't limit myself to the one page - not initially anyway. In order for me to really allow my thoughts to flow, I just had to write and get all of my thoughts down on paper. I wrote the responses to the questions in my first drafts without space limitations. I then went back and really looked at the job descriptions and considered the dimensions set in the instructions and edited my final response accordingly. The examination process could include any of the following and others:

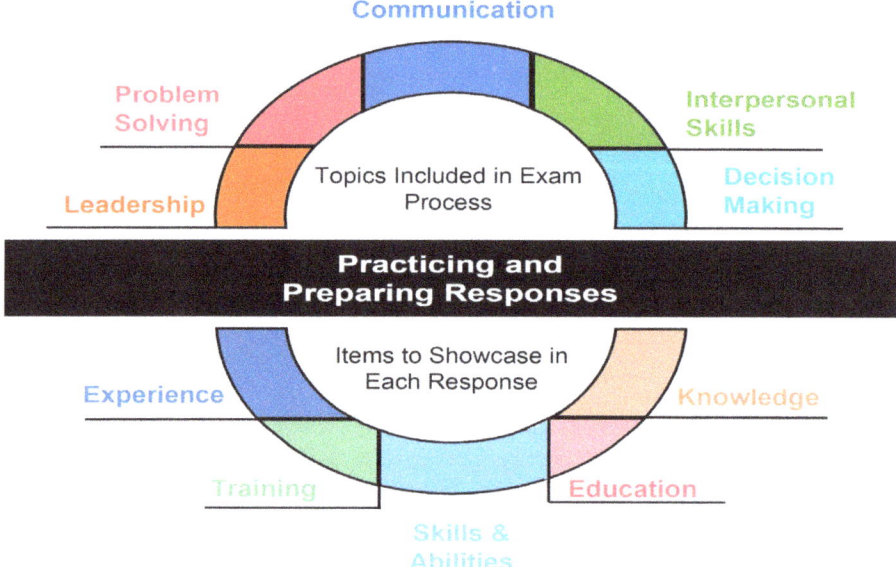

(**Note:** these can often be found in assessment center type examination processes). In my final response, I made certain to showcase my experience, training, education, knowledge, skills, and abilities that painted a picture of readiness for promotion.

Make sure to include relevant context to describe the level of your role and responsibility in your assignment. For example:

Prompt Question: "What are your qualifications for this position?" Instead of responding, "I supervised a team in the ABC Unit" consider saying, "I supervised 25 personnel responsible for statewide coordination of safety programs and had oversight for a multi-million dollar budget." The second response gives more depth, detail and life to your words to help the evaluator assess your ability and readiness for the position.

Basically, it is best to cut out all the fluff. Although it is a preparation exercise, you will appreciate the outcome after you put yourself through it. Make sure to ANSWER the question as you're crafting your response around all the above. Remember to use good sentence structure, formatting with a short opening, body of main points to address the prompt and short closing. Be concise and then…put the pen down or turn off the computer. You are done with those.

See ANNEX RESOURCES for examples of written prompts.

So, what are you waiting for? Waiting is not just sitting around hoping that you passed the written exam. While you're in the waiting period, you should be preparing for the next step in the process.

Chapter 5

Preparing for the Oral Panel Interview

By now, it may seem like there is no break in sight, and well, you're right. So, with your study mindset still humming from the preparation for the written exam, let's keep the momentum going. Some examination processes will have a quick turnaround and others may have a much longer turnaround before the next phase of the process. For the oral panel interview component, you will follow a very similar format for your study sessions from Chapter 3 relative to the frequency of your most recent study patterns. HOWEVER, the way you will study this material will be very different.

Survival Guide

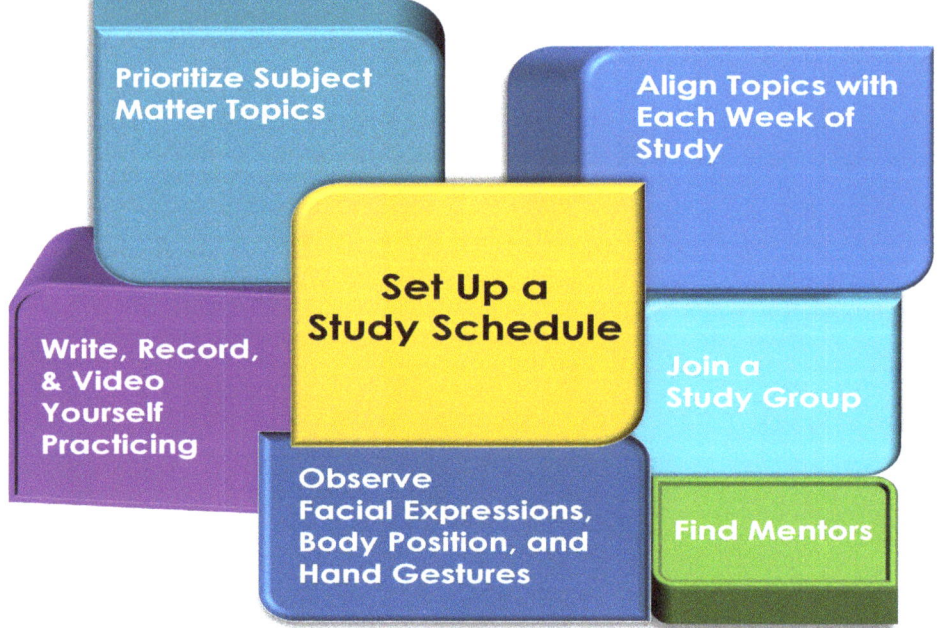

Set Up a Study Routine and Schedule

    Let's take it one step at a time so that it will be crystal clear. As you did for the Written Test, you will need to set up a study schedule with all of your prioritized subject matter topics identified for each week of study. We will talk about what type of topics you will consider in just a minute. Understanding your learning style is important, so plan on what works best for you. When I was preparing for my various oral interviews, I wrote, recorded and videoed myself for most of my preparation processes. It is always a good laugh to see yourself on video, or hear your own voice. Wow! But really, it helped me notice things like saying "uh," or "um," or "like" and to observe my facial expressions, body position and/or hand gesturing.

    Again, I recommend getting into a study group of some kind so that you can gain from a broader learning environment and receive information from those in higher positions that are willing to share information and help you be successful. I found there weren't always many of those study groups available, and the ones that were had secret handshakes in order to get into them. So, what did I do you ask? You are asking, aren't you? Well, since I wasn't in the "inner" circle of trust, I found my own mentors to help me. Once I was in management, I found a great role model who invited me to a study group.

This study group was amazing! That is where I truly learned the value of networking, learning from others and how to really prepare for the examination processes. As I moved up in the organization, I was inspired and began making sure that there was always a study workshop for my staff that didn't need a secret handshake to gain entrance - only a willingness to sacrifice your time and commitment to the group.

Study Topics: What Should You Focus On?

Now, let's talk about topics for your study plan. One thing I found that worked nicely was to first create a list of 12-15 topic areas around which you would begin building your study material. Depending on your organization, your topics may vary, but I will try to illustrate through an example the breadth of subjects that may be relevant:

- Agency head vision statements
- Mission/Organizational Values/Professional Values
- Employee Wellness
- Equal Employment Opportunity (EEO)
- Budget/Fiscal Accountability
- Civil Liability
- Employee Misconduct/Personnel Issues–Progressive Discipline
- Bargaining Unit/Union/Associations
- Strategic Plan
- Contemporary Incidents that have occurred in your industry, your organization (i.e. law enforcement: social unrest, community and police relations; legislative changes; critical incidents; use of force)
- Community Engagement
- Recruitment, Retention and Succession Planning
- Injury and Illness Case Management
- Employee substance abuse
- Employee morale

This list is not all inclusive; rather, it's an example of the type of study material topics you may want to begin preparing for this portion of the examination process. See ANNEX RESOURCES for additional examples.

Pay close attention to what the executive management of your organization is discussing at their meetings, as that information should be available and is usually disseminated through the chain of command. Meet with your supervisor or manager and simply ask what relevant topics you should study and prepare for and what is important for you to know about them.

If possible, reach out to subject matter experts that can help narrow your focus on the hot topic issues they are facing in their shops. Again, they may also have prepared some talking points or study packets for applicants that contain some general information to help you. Whatever the subject matter is, remember that you need to understand the topic as it relates to the examination and the responsibilities outlined in the examination bulletin.

As you study the material, review the policy surrounding it, look specifically at the responsibility of the position you are seeking AND make sure you know the responsibility of the position below it as you'll be responsible for that as well. Create some short outlines of information you can easily refer to as you condense your study over the last few weeks before the oral panel interviews.

Creating Study Scenarios

Sometimes it is helpful to create scenarios for yourself around the topics under consideration so that you can begin to formulate your response style. Scenarios involve creating a hypothetical situation or issue that you may have to address. In order to resolve that situation or issue you would have to draw upon your background, training, and experience.

When working through scenario questions, you will need to develop a strategy in order to be able to provide a well-rounded response. Some people who are studying for examinations create acronyms which help them to remember information and have a systematic approach to responses. See ANNEX RESOURCES for additional examples.

> **Case Study Scenario**
>
> You have a subordinate employee that was seen harassing one of the clerical employees. One of your other subordinate employees comes to you, the supervisor, to let you know. What is your role and what action should you take?

I do recommend preparing your response strategies in a way that no matter how the question is asked in the examination you will feel prepared to answer it comfortably.

First, always know policy. Period. You must then consider the question and make sure you understand what's being asked of you. Assess or analyze the scenario dynamics. Prepare your response without a lot of fluff. Be concise, informative, and clear.

Here's a basic example of a scenario and an appropriate response strategy:

- What is policy? – Cover your departmental EEO policy

- What is your role? – Understand and know both your role and expectations as well as that of your employees

- What action will you take? Consider all of your options but stay in line with policy guidelines. Add any other additional information that would be good and relative to any employee assistance, follow up, training, and/or discussions with all of the staff on EEO policy.

- Remember to be specific as to how you will handle both the employee who was harassed, the employee that did the harassing, and the witnesses that might have observed the incident.

- Are you familiar with external processes afforded to your employee for filing an EEO claim? What considerations have you given to the overall work environment? Who do you need to notify? Did you advise everyone involved on EEO policy? Is there any internal investigation taking place? Did you consider employee rights during our contacts? Did you make proper management notifications? Will any final documentation be necessary?

On all scenarios always consider who is impacted (internal and external stakeholders), who needs to know, what they need to know, closing documentation, follow up and training issues or needs and are there any correlations to other policy, strategic plan, mission, etc. See ANNEX RESOURCES for additional strategies and techniques.

Usually, this portion of the process is timed, so be cognizant of your time limits. For example, you may get 5 or 6 questions and have 45 minutes to answer them ALL. So, if you use 15 minutes on one question, well, you do the math.

Some examinations also will add disruptive elements like a panel member who will make a statement or ask a question of you while you are in the middle of your response. Try not to get rattled and acknowledge them with a brief response and then redirect your focus back to making sure you address the question. This sounds easy, but it can be very distracting.

For example, let's say your scenario or question is a community engagement topic. You are in the middle of explaining the programs, vision, and strategic plan when out of the blue one of the panelists says, "What are you doing about the homelessness in my neighborhood?" What will be your response? More than likely you will begin to address the question with policy and procedures, but don't forget to consider the humanistic approach on how you should treat people. Try to include resources, programs, training and other connected community support groups that partner with your agency in order that you might give a well-rounded response.

Preparing for the Oral Panel Interview

Remember, the oral panel interview process is to evaluate your readiness for promotion and the examination can be inclusive of a variety of styles. Get to know the history or your agency's processes and be prepared for it.

The oral panel interview study time frame can be anywhere from a week or two to an 8-10 week commitment. Around the midway point in your study schedule, set up opportunities to conduct mini mock oral panel interviews with mentors or leadership in the agency to see how your preparation is going. Make sure to request feedback and take notes or ask them to take notes they can subsequently provide to you. Other suggestions can include either recording yourself or doing a video of yourself during these mock panel interviews.

Another recommendation is to find out who the panel interviewers will be for your examination and on your panel. Why? I feel it never hurts to know who you're going to interview with and who will be assessing you. Your audience matters.

Generally, the panel is made up of representatives from your agency and maybe someone from outside of it such as an HR person, an equivalent rank or classification from another agency or even community members. Panels will be made up of 2-4 people. Make sure to make eye contact with all of the panelists at ALL times. Do not be distracted if they are writing, NOT writing or even if they are showing absolutely NO facial expressions at all. Most HR departments do not allow panelists to be engaged, encouraging or discouraging to candidates. There's something about keeping the examination environment fair and consistent - or more like intimidating.

Remember, it's an oral panel interview process, so TALK! Even if you're cerebrally problem solving your way through it, say it out loud. The panel can't hear what you're thinking. You should be conversational. Do not be rigid. Try not to sound like you're going through a checklist of information. While a checklist may be a great study tool to help remember the steps in the process, you certainly don't want to sound like you're reading one. You are attempting to share all that you have been studying along with your life and work experience up to this point. It will be best if all of it can be presented in a concise, well-organized and well-prepared way.

Here's an example of the steps you should consider when framing a response during an oral panel interview:

- Review the questions carefully.
- Role: Address question from your ROLE for the position.
- Response Actions: Yours, staff, assisting resources, stakeholders.
- Policy: Know your agency policy on the topic and apply it.
- Processes: Explain the process within the policy. It will often provide the answer to the question. Details matter versus generalizing.
- Documentation: Reporting is required in most instances. Consider the actual forms, timelines, information needed and where the information is to be submitted.
- Notifications: Notifications can be immediate, during and after. It's important to identify who needs to be notified and what information you are providing in the notification within your role. Additionally, think of not only notifying up your chain of command but peers, allied partners, and external stakeholders that need to be identified as well.
  What additional specialized resources are needed?
- Training: Identify what training policy is relative to the question or scenario. Training includes previous training that would have been required along with training that may be needed as a refresher course, developmental training or as disciplinary action to improve performance.
- Follow up: What follow up needs to be conducted? What does policy say? Think internally and externally, organizationally, and individually.
  Follow up also includes monitoring and setting hard times to regroup with staff to reassess outcomes.

These are just a few suggestions on how to navigate specific response strategies. See ANNEX RESOURCES for additional examples, strategies and techniques.

Recommend the day before the exam:

- Try to sleep
- Try not to study
- Limit who you're talking to so you don't get overwhelmed.

Day of the Oral Panel Interview is GAME DAY. You are ON. Let's get this!

CHAPTER 6

GAME DAY

It's here!

The DAY which you have been preparing for – for either two days or two years has arrived. Did you actually get any sleep last night? I know I did the first time I took my first promotional examination. Why? Because I had no idea what was involved or what to expect. I honestly felt that I should have been able to walk right in and take the exam that I knew nothing about because I felt that I was pretty smart and that would be enough. So, I slept like a baby and went right in there and failed it.

Survival Guide

What's Your Plan for GAME DAY?

But, for you, this is GAME DAY. What is this day all about for you? Prior to a big game, most professional athletes try to find sanctuary, whatever that may be for each of them. That sanctuary helps them to calm their nerves and settle in before the big game. If you tend to worry, or become overly nervous, find some comfort in your routine. Go about doing what you would normally do as far as exercise, eating breakfast, meditating, showering, and singing your favorite tune. Make sure you give yourself ample time to get through all of your activities. You don't want to feel rushed at any point and add stress to your stress.

I remember my GAME DAY for my Captain's examination. It was an assessment center process which I had never done before so the testing environment was going to be very different than any of the other exams I had taken previously. We weren't required to be in uniform so we could wear business attire. I had everything all set out the night before so I didn't have to think about what I was going to wear the morning of the big day. However, what I hadn't considered was that I had purchased the new suit I was going to wear three months earlier. Yep, three whole months earlier because I saw it on sale, loved it, and so I bought it. Well, needless to say I'm feeling good, things are moving right along, and then I go to put the pants on and…well, they didn't fit. Immediately my "fight or flight" response kicked in, beads of sweat started to develop and my heart started beating faster as I began to panic. After a little of the fog had cleared, I remembered that I still had other suits that fit and that I could wear. It wasn't as I planned, but it would work just fine and no one would know but me that it had even happened.

I am sharing this small moment of stress to highlight the importance of assessing your emotional readiness for successfully surviving the long process of promotional examination preparation and the sometimes even longer journey of actual promotions. Study after study shows the impact of releasing stress hormones through the "fight or flight" response physiologically, psychologically and physically. Chronic stress can contribute to anxiety, depression, addictions, obesity, and significant other health issues. Although it has evolved as a survival mechanism for life-threatening moments, it has become a default response for everyday stressors that include work issues, family problems, traffic delays, promotional examinations and the big promotion itself. Therefore, make time to find ways to manage and cope with the nuances of your stressful moments. And do not allow yourself to get stumped by the little things that will come up and throw you off your game. Work through it, breathe and then keep it moving.

Getting to the Exam and Then What Happens?

Arrive early (way early if you need to) for the examination. This will give you time to avoid any traffic snafus. Rethink parking and how far you might have to walk in inclement or hot weather. There's nothing like being either a wet or melted applicant who is breathing heavy once you get inside. Familiarize yourself with the waiting area by going to the restroom and re-check your optics. Yes, make sure you don't look disheveled. Are you ruffled? Sweaty? Get a drink of water or coffee, say hello to people versus just going to check in and sitting like a statue until you're called.

It actually helped me a lot to make others feel more comfortable when we were in those environments. Maybe it's not always just about ourselves in these moments before the examination. You know, those moments where we get so bottled up inside our own heads trying to remember all the information that we've been studying that we forget to be decent to the other people around us. We guard ourselves almost as though we are amongst the enemy – those same poor souls who are waiting to go in and endure the same torture we are about to experience. If you can, try to relax. Take some deep breaths and casually talk with others sitting around you. Of course only if they are open to it. They may be having their own inner battle and are at a loss for words, so don't take it personal. Sometimes by helping others we really can help ourselves.

Time passes slowly, and then quickly. They call your name. It's ok, you are ready. You are prepared. Go in and handle your business. Make sure you shake hands and greet the panelists, interviewers, or assessors. Body language is important. Smile, be friendly, have good posture and make consistent eye contact. Basically, be confident that you are where you are supposed to be because you deserve to be there. It's also about using your inner voice to talk yourself up in your own head. Remember, YOU HAVE PREPARED and YOU ARE PREPARED!

Make sure to pay attention to the instructions:

- Is the examination timed? If so, how much time do you have? Where is the timer, clock, or your watch so you can monitor?

- Are the questions given to you so you can read along? Remember to listen to them as they read each question. Feel free to take time to re-read the question after they do if you need to-that's why they gave you a copy.

- Are the questions 2 or 3 part questions? Consider what you're going to say before you blurt out and just start talking. Stick to your preparation and your plan of approach for the topic or questions.

- REMEMBER YOUR TRAINING (STUDY) PREPARATION! Don't feel rushed. Pace yourself so you don't spend too much time on any one question. Look up and check your timer or watch.

- Try to maintain eye contact with each panel person - not just the one that asked you the question. When you're finished with a question, let the panel know verbally so they can clearly move on to the next question.

- What if there is a planned disruption by a panel member or role player that asks you a question or makes a statement while you are giving a response? Respond reasonably and naturally as you would if it was really happening to you. If possible, address the disruption briefly and state that you can share more with them after the meeting and/or presentation, etc. Segue as quickly as possible back to addressing the original question. Sometimes you can still answer the question through the interaction with the role player. Just don't forget to stay focused on the question in the prompt.

Remember to close out your interview with a thank you or handshake. Unless your panel offers you a closing, don't worry about having one. Closings have a lot less importance than they may have in the past because of the type of scoring considerations for the examination process. Gather yourself and walk gracefully out the door, out of the building and get into your vehicle. Exhale. You did it.

Half the battle was just showing up. You did that! Feel good about your win and proud of your accomplishment.

Finishing the Exam and Managing Your Emotions

But wait, all of a sudden you are starting to replay the interview or assessment center through your head again. You are beating yourself up because you didn't say this or you should have said that. Oh wait, maybe that was just me every time I finished an examination.

I remember as I was driving back from my assistant chief examination that I became so rattled as I ruminated over the exam because I had forgotten to add something to one of my responses that really wasn't even relevant. But at that particular moment, I was mentally battling it out and going through everything that had just transpired. So, what did I do? I called another candidate who had taken the test earlier and we started talking. As he was sharing what he said, I felt even worse because I hadn't said any of what he was saying and I immediately started doubting as to whether I had done well at all on the test.

The trouble is rumination leads you to think about those things that increase negative aspects of the situation versus the positive ones when you're stressed or distressed, and you use them to interpret your understanding of what's happening in the moment. This will not do you any good as it can make things pessimistically distorted, and you end up caught in the tangle of rumination making you feel worse.

My point is to allow yourself time to go through a range of emotions. Some candidates will feel confident that they did well. Some candidates may feel they had fallen short. Some candidates may feel like, "What just happened?" Just know that it is all normal -very normal. Give yourself time to decompress. However, don't ruminate indefinitely. Rumination is another arm of the "fight or flight" stress response release, and as a result, your brain and body are flooded with the stress hormone cortisol when you're in rumination mode.

To avoid the health hazards that can accompany rumination which mirror those mentioned earlier, is to become aware of when you're doing it. We often feel like we are going back over the moment in a problem-solving way when we are really ruminating, chewing on it over and over until we get lost in the negativity. Therefore, it's important to give yourself the time to have those emotions but limit them. Then find a way to disrupt the cycle of thinking that begins to overwhelm you by taking a walk, listen to your favorite song, go spend time with your family or a good friend.

Regaining control of your thoughts and emotions is important and it puts you back in the right frame of mind to handle the rest of the process.

I would recommend limiting who you briefly touch base with after the examination. Consider texting those few "need to notify" people to say that you've finished and that you'll reach out to them later. Try to give yourself some space. When you feel you're ready, then engage. But do it very carefully. If you get into too many discussions about specifics with your fellow examinees or anyone else for that matter, it can possibly get you into trouble as you should have signed a little paper about confidentiality. Don't get yourself into trouble, stick to the RULES.

Secondly, too many discussions will have you second guessing yourself over and over. In many instances, it takes weeks for the results of these examinations to come out. I would hate for you to sit around pushing rewind for weeks. It's agonizing and unnecessary. The bottom line is you've already tested. YOU CANNOT CHANGE THAT. GAME DAY is a wrap!

CHAPTER 7

RESULTS DAY

Hmm, when do you get your results? The estimated date when the results' list would be provided should have been in your examination bullet in. Sometimes, if you work at a smaller agency, the panel will just let you know when to expect notification. Let's just take our time while we navigate this moment. You are either going to get a call first or you will simply get your notice in the mail. Someone may even have seen a promotional list before you even know it's out and give you a call. The bottom line is that you'll get notified one way or the other.

At the Top
Consider the pros and cons - location, cost to your family, lifestyle, health, wallet, commutes, etc. before submitting for a promotional role.

In the Middle
Can be the sweet zone. No pressure to promote quickly, but you may need to conduct oral interview process again.

At the Bottom
Stay positive and informed on how promotions are going and keep your eye out for opportunities.

Not on the List
Don't get discouraged.
Feel your feelings, get back on the horse and get ready for another exam round.

Survival Guide

What Happens if I'm at the Top, Middle, Bottom or not on the List?

Before you get to the point of knowing where you are on the list, the question for you to be prepared for is what if you're at the top of the list, middle, bottom or not on the list at all? Have you taken the time to consider any of this? Well, I'll just let you in on a little secret, it doesn't matter what you think you're going to feel because your response to any of it is going to be all over the page.

With that in mind, what if you're at the top? Wow, the feeling is overwhelming. You are shocked, excited, and then it suddenly begins to creep in again. What creeps in you ask? The questions... Those questions of where will I promote? When will I promote? Am I ready for this? Oh, goodness, I AM ACTUALLY GOING TO PROMOTE!

As you're going through this range of emotions there are some things to consider:

- What is your department's hiring guidelines for those who are promoting?

- Is the next step an interview with a chief, a head of agency, or a manager?

- What offers will be available if you are to go to a field versus an administrative assignment?

- Is it a "rule of three" eligibility on a list for your ability to put in for a position? What does that even mean?

- Do you understand what you need to do to be considered for open positions?

- Are you prepared to go anywhere or take any assignment?

- Does your process penalize you if you pass up an offer in order to wait on other opportunities?

- Do you put in for the first open positions? If so, why or why not? What are the consequences?

- How do I need to leverage my network relationships?

If You're at the Top… Those fortunate enough to score well and end up at the top of a promotional list are both instantly excited and worried all at the same time. I suggest you consider the consequences of your excitement and enthusiasm before you put in for anything and everything as a result of being at the top of the list. Yes, there are benefits of getting your seniority clock ticking in the position so that you can work your way to a cushy assignment or something closer to home if you have to promote far away. However, what is the cost to your family, your lifestyle, your health and your wallet if you have to commute or move your family to an entirely different city? Remember those questions in the first chapter?

For those in city, municipal or county agencies, you might not have to deal with distance as a factor but there may be other concerns that need to be carefully evaluated. Federal and state agencies have many variables as well, including geography.

When I accepted my first promotion as a sergeant, I had two small children and a husband who was a police officer with a local department. Working graveyards many nights while the kids were young, studying while they were in school, and handling family obligations before going to work was tough. I couldn't imagine, or rather, I didn't really think about what would happen if I promoted and had to commute or ask my family to move. I was fortunate and got an opportunity to promote about 45 minutes from home which was a reasonable commute.

Promotions will take a toll emotionally, physically and in ways you may not realize until years later. Therefore, it is so important to address the questions in Chapter 1 so that you can establish a foundation, support and a platform for your overall success in this journey.

If You're at the Bottom… What if you're at the bottom of the list? What does that mean for you? Well, depending on the size of your agency or how your promotions are projected to happen over the next year or two, it could be fine. On the other hand, you could be right on the bubble of opportunity. I recommend staying as positive as possible. Always stay informed on how promotions are going and keep your eye out for opportunities.

Things you might want to consider while you're waiting:

- Remember Chapters 1 and 2. Go back to these chapters and see where you can begin working on strengthening some of the areas discussed in them. Assess the need to seek out special projects or assignments; educational or training opportunities and places you can get more community engagement and outreach exposure.

- Continue planning for how you will need to adjust when you promote.

- As the list moves along and you see that there may not be an opportunity, should you begin to prepare for the process again? I would consider this if it has been 6 months or so prior to another examination being posted.

- Keep all your study material organized, brush off your application and keep it handy.

- Go back to your examination results' notice and look at the breakdown of your results to see where you can improve your score. Where was your greatest weakness? Was it the written portion or the oral panel interview? Could it have been the writing assignment? Or the resume? What portion of your preparation needs work for the assessment center?

- If possible, get feedback from the panel.

Don't get discouraged if the positions on your list are passing by and you haven't been promoted yet. Your list may even be close to expiring. However, to give you some context, baby boomers will be retiring at a rate of 10,000 per day over the next 10 years and employment decisions for all fields of endeavor have shifted significantly as a result of the pandemic we experienced in 2020. The same turnover that affects the private sector impacts the law enforcement and public safety sector as well. It would be wise to monitor your organizational trends which you can easily deduce from those retiring monthly or annually. Each of those numbers translates into vacancies. There is always opportunity, whether as a result of this examination or the next. Stay prepared.

Listen, I have been at the bottom of the list twice and not on the list at all twice. The first one was that third chance at the sergeant's exam. I was number 123 out of 125. The bottom line in all of this was even though I was at the bottom of that list, I STILL promoted. The second time I was at the bottom of the list was the first time I took the captain's exam. I wanted to stay viable, so I took it again. The next time, I prepared differently for GAME DAY and I was in the top rank. The two times I didn't make the list at all, I wasn't prepared or ready. I think that pretty much says it all, don't you?

In the Middle of the List... Did I forget to mention anything about the middle? Well, the middle can really be the sweet zone. There's no pressure to make some quick decision and you really don't have to be too worried about not getting an opportunity. You can use this position on the list to carefully plan and prepare for the promotion. Remember, the only caveat will be that you'll have to begin to prepare for an interview if required by your internal hiring guidelines.

Not on the List... I didn't want to leave this chapter without acknowledging strategies for those who don't find themselves on the promotional list. Don't get discouraged. It sounds easy to say, and I know how disappointing it feels. However, after you allow yourself to go through the range of emotions, feeling embarrassed, angry, frustrated, sad and disjointed, it will be time to get back on the horse and go for another ride. The luxury of taking an examination a second or third time is you that have an advantage that the first time test takers don't have. You know what to expect and you know where you need to improve. Your exam results will help you identify your areas that need improvement. Pay attention to the information in that piece of paper.

As I've mentioned before, in the examinations where I didn't test well, I didn't put in the effort. There was no discipline, structure, or commitment by me. Anything worth achieving will take more than we want to give most of the time. Trust me, while it may look easy to some, most of those having success are putting in hours you never get to see. Most professional athletes are putting in 30-40 hours a week or more. The Olympic swimmer, Michael Phelps practiced every single day in the pool for three to six hours and then did other exercises outside of the pool four to five days a week.

It's not over until you decide it's over. What I discovered through my ride on the roller coaster of promotional processes is that I had to evolve. I learned to have patience in my wait and lean into it. While in that wait, I continued to learn and be competent in the position that I was in – always trying to getting better. It is of the utmost importance to stay qualified and always invest in you. It's up to you, but I would consider that you recalibrate, refresh your material, and get your plan in place.

As a reminder, be careful of the perpetual spin of promotions. You can feel like your entire career has been one big cycle of study, promote, study, fail, study, promote for 15-20 years. If that's your chosen path, plan for the marathon and not the race. Remember, the importance of your physical, physiological, and psychological health throughout the journey.

CHAPTER 8

IT'S ALL OVER. OR IS IT?

By now, you've settled in a bit to the reality that the testing process has come to a close, at least, for now. What does "for now" mean? Well, it really depends on you.

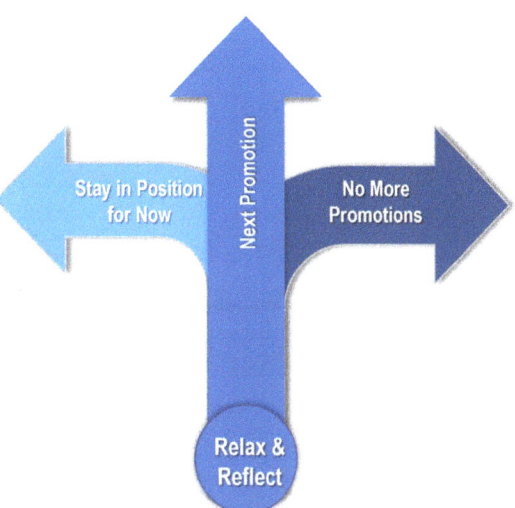

For many of you, after going through the gauntlet of preparation, you are probably packing away the study material and putting it in a far, far away place. Or maybe you simply did the after-study dump right into the "confidential" shredder. For others, you are deciding if you should retake a test or begin to prepare for the next promotional step on the ladder. The only recommendations that I will really make in this closing chapter is for you to take some time and reflect on how you felt going through this last examination promotional process. Things you might consider asking yourself:

- Was it even worth all the time and energy?

- What did I have to personally compromise to study for the examination?

- Was my family on board throughout the process? How did they feel? How do they feel now?

- Why do I even want to promote again? Is it for the money, or is it something more?

- Am I able to be resilient enough after each of these examination processes or the promotions? How is my overall mental health after the experience?

- Did I feel like my agency was supportive in the process for promotion?

- Have I created a strong network of mentors, coaches, and other allies to help me be successful in future promotions?

These are only a fraction of the type of questions to consider asking yourself and your family before you make your decision. For me, I wasn't initially driven by evaluating these types of questions because I didn't really know what I was getting myself into until I was in it. It wasn't until my lieutenant's promotion, or even my captain's promotion, that I really began to understand the importance of giving consideration to the questions listed above. If I had reassessed my own understanding of the "why" I was promoting, I might have taken a different path, or waited at different times.

However, with that said, I am a true believer that there are no coincidences. The path we are on is the one we must learn to navigate, and I navigated it the best way I could. My successes and failures are symbiotic in a way, as one without the other does not determine my balance of growth, my acquisition of knowledge, or my greater purpose and contribution to others and the industry.

The great thing about the freedom to take a promotional examination is simply that, you are free to take it or not. But remember:

- Don't allow others to pressure you into taking an examination you are not ready for and don't allow yourself to pressure yourself either way.

- Be humble in your assessment of how to move forward with a healthy balance of boldness.

- Have confidence in yourself, work hard and take action.

- Remember, time will either pass you by, or you can jump in and do something with it.

It's All Over. Or Is It?

For those who successfully promote into their next position the level of freedom changes. You are now responsible for leading others in your organization and that requires much more than it took for you to pass the examination. Remember, your leadership will always be evolving but do your best to be inspiring, engaging, motivational while doing all you can to increase your emotional intelligence quotient. Leadership is not a luxury, it's selfless sacrifice.

Keep these tips in your toolbox of new leadership:
1. Be an authentic leader and have integrity.
2. Who you are is how you lead, truly.
3. Set expectations well above mediocrity and live up to them.
4. Make sure you deliver on the commitments you make.
5. Value and invest in your people, including yourself.
6. Have the courage to always stand for what's right.

This ends this literal and figurative chapter of your promotional preparation journey. Once you actually promote, that will begin an entirely different survival guide. It is all your decision, so choose wisely.

Best of luck to you and remember to always reach back, across and up to enrich the quality of the profession and your own leadership and to spark inspiration in the next person!

ANNEX

RESOURCES

Survival Guide

ANNEX A

CAREER DEVELOPMENT PLAN

Step 1: Write down any of your most important career interests.

PRIMARY CAREER INTEREST: Reach the level (rank) of Executive Management

Step 2: Identify long-term professional goals (including positions desired within the organization).

Long-term professional goals: (You can even set actual goal dates you want to achieve the positions)
   1. Promote to Sergeant or Supervisor (Year)
   2. Promote to Lieutenant or Manager (Year)
   3. Promote to Captain or Commander (Year)

Step 3: Identify any short-term goals that will contribute to long-term interests/assignments.
Short-term professional goals:
   1. Be an acting supervisor or manager
   2. Be a team leader for a special assignment or project
   3. Join external community organizations

Step 4: List 2-3 activities that will help you reach each goal. Specify how you will accomplish the activities. Include what steps to take in order to reach the goals. Include any resources you might need, and when you will start and finish it. (Name as many as you want, this is just a short example).

Career development activities:
Short-term Goal 1: Be an acting supervisor or manager.

Activity: Seek out training that builds supervisory or management skills in order to be selected as an acting (in charge) supervisor or manager on an intermittent or interim basis.

How to accomplish: You must let those in charge know that you are interested in an opportunity and when asked, accommodate the request.

Cultivate good working relationships with those you work for, those you work with and those you will oversee.

Starting date: Pick a date and **GET STARTED.**

Date of completion: Keep it open unless you have decided on a designated timeframe.

Short-term Goal 2: Be a team leader for a special assignment or project.

Activity: Make yourself available for extra assignments outside of your regular work duties.

How to accomplish: Again, let those in charge of you know you are interested in participating in attending community events; working on internal administrative projects; being a part of a committee; being a mentor for a new employee; and when asked, accommodate the requests.

Starting date: RIGHT NOW (Ok, or set a date that works for you).

Date of completion: Leave open unless you have a designated timeframe.

Short-term Goal 3: Join external community organizations.

Activity: Actively seek out community organizations that will get you involved in local or national community contributions.

How to accomplish: Begin by selecting an organization that is local and maybe you're familiar with like your church, rotary, or a nonprofit. The organization you join can be interwoven into the work you do for your profession and can have mutual benefits as you build trust and bridge gaps between the community partnership and your organization.

Starting date: Anytime.
Date of completion: Ongoing.

Step 5: Write down any additional skills, knowledge or experience you would like to acquire that may directly or indirectly help you in your

current or future positions.

Additional skills, knowledge, experience desired:

1. Increase knowledge of technology programs within the organization

2. Enroll in training courses: conflict management, problem solving, analytical skills, and/or leadership

3. Complete educational goals: AA, BA, BS, MA, MS, Ph.D

Step 6: Identify when you will meet with your supervisor or manager and what will be discussed. Progress report meetings:

Progress Meeting 1: Meeting with manager
Date and Time: Monday August 5, 10:00 a.m.
Purpose: Discuss opportunity to attend a community panel discussion
Progress Meeting 2: Phone call with manager
Date and Time: Friday September 7, 10:00 a.m.
Purpose: Address relevant learning from training class

NOTE: This Career Development Plan can look as complex or simple as you choose. The importance is that you have one and you use it as a guide for your career goals.

ANNEX B
EXAMPLE OF A 10-WEEK PROMOTIONAL WRITTEN EXAMINATION STUDY GROUP PLAN
(In-Person and Virtual)
One Session a week for the written test
(Example is for police sergeant)

Materials Needed: General Orders, Management Memorandums, Standard Operating Procedures, Patrol Manuals, Patrol Guides, Peace Officers Legal Source Book, laws, codes – relevant material for the examination.

WEEK 1: (VERY IMPORTANT TO SET THE CADENCE)

1. Set expectations for the study group. Treat your study group like an actual academic class. Attendees need to show up prepared to take notes and engage in class discussions. Make sure to cover the examination bulletin or announcement to highlight the scope of knowledge, skills and abilities required and ensure they meet the minimum qualification (MQ) requirements to apply for the exam:

- Do they meet the minimum requirements (time on, field/administrative split, what other requirements, time in current position if for a manager and above).

2. Did they complete the application properly and in a timely fashion? Ensure that they meet the MQs on the application and follow all the directions. It is their responsibility to make sure the application gets to the HR department, or designated location for timely filing submission. Follow the instructions on whether it can be hand delivered or if it is being mailed, consider a secured delivery so it will arrive before the post mark date specified in the bulletin or announcement.

3. Go over the scope of the examination bulletin and dates that are in it. Spend about 30 minutes on this portion.

4. Explain to the students the best strategies on how to study for optimal retention and understanding:
    a. Read policy/material and create short concise outlines.
    b. Create 3x5 cards for easy access to go over information.
    c. Verbally record information for audio listening.
    d. Identify technology that can be used in developing and creating quizzes.
    e. Discuss the process of prioritizing what to study.

5. Go over the entire 10-week schedule, create a schedule, and provide to the students. Assign the first three manuals and go over a few chapters within to demonstrate how to review and highlight.

6. Explain and assign weekly the creation of at least 20-25 quiz questions and answers and have them submit electronically before the next session. From those questions, you (the facilitator) create a quiz bank of all the questions. Use this bank of questions and answers for weekly quizzes, mid-term, final, or as study material in the final study document.

WEEK 2:
Take the quiz first. Grade the quiz and only keep the correct answers. Move into covering the next three manuals and related material. The facilitator should remind students to make sure policies are updated and current. Many agencies have a process for updating policy so that you don't have to go through an extensive process. Assign study material reading, review week 1 and create questions and answers. Study stacking is essential each week.

Repeat this process until week 5.

WEEK 5: Mid-term.

Start the class with the mid-term, between 50-75 questions from the first 5 weeks. Score the exam and keep only the right answers. Answers should only be verbatim from policy. Assign the next week's homework and task to create questions and answers.

Repeat this process from weeks 1-4 until week 9.

WEEK 9: Final Exam.

This practice exam should be at least 100-110 questions. The students should be given 4 hours to take the exam (or match the time allocations for the particular exam guidelines for your agency). This can also be a take home exam and encourage them to practice as though they were in the testing environment. Score exam and keep only the correct answers.

All materials should have been reviewed, discussed, or quizzed on by this week. Facilitator (you) should prepare a final preparation document that is a collection of all the quizzes with **ONLY THE CORRECT ANSWERS,** any relevant updates condensed for ease of understanding, and some key elements from policy captured in one FINAL document for study. *The final document can be from 50-100 pages depending on how much information you've consolidated.

Note: Students may carry around a large binder through most of the process until the final weeks. When they get down to the last couple of weeks, it should become a condensed final study document.

WEEK 10: Students (you) should take a few days to study and then a couple of days prior to try to relax, especially the day before the exam. On the morning of, hydrate, relax and go take the test.

ANNEX C

ORAL PANEL INTERVIEW
STUDY WORKSHOP FORMAT

ORAL PANEL INTERVIEW PREPARATION

Pre-Workshop Considerations

When setting up the schedule for the Panel Interview Study Workshop, consider the following:

- Should it be held virtually, in-person or as a hybrid?

- If in-person, consider all of the logistics involved including travel to the location for those living farther away and room for the number of attending.

- Identify subject matter experts (SMEs) that can speak to your study group on the pertinent subjects directly (EEO, Internal Affairs, Human Resources, Risk Management, Budget, etc). Make sure to:
    - Schedule them in advance and give the speakers/presenters guidelines to follow. They need to understand the topic, discuss the policy and the role of the position for which you are being tested, explain expectations, and provide examples/scenarios. It's also helpful if they can provide practical applications and policy driven information in a systematic approach so the students can directly correlate to policy.

    - Speakers, presenters, and SMEs should make sure to include the connectivity to professional values, employee assistance and wellness programs for employees, training requirements, documentation, notification, and any additional considerations for follow up. Think about who is impacted in the scenario, internally/externally? Future implications or considerations? Does it correlate to other policy, a strategic plan or mission?

Create panel interview topics that will be helpful for the workshops:

Identify 12-15 "Hot" topics and other relevant topics that might be in the examination: Strategic Plan, Chief's Vision Statement, Organizational Mission and Values, Civil Liability, EEO, Budget Process & Planning, use of force incidents, personnel issues, resource allocations, social unrest, pandemic response, etc.

Plan the schedule based on the duration of your study workshop and explain the time commitments along with the agenda, if possible.

DURATION: 8-10 Weeks depending on the examination cycle of your agency.

WEEKLY SESSION COMMITMENT: Each week should contain ONE session of about 90 MINUTES in length.

Each week two or three topics should be covered per session depending on the amount of study content. *Creating a reasonable balance in workload for the study workshop will help you and the other students to not feel too overwhelmed.

MIDPOINT: Week 5 conduct informal mini mock interviews within the study group. Create mock questions/scenarios. Divided into groups of 3 or 4 students that will rotate within their group: interviewer, evaluator, or observer. After each round, each member of the group will provide feedback. Rotate so that each student has a turn at each position.

LAST SESSION: Coordinate formal mock interviews for the candidates and solicit volunteers to assist on the panels. Try to make it as close to the real testing environment as possible. If candidates need to be in uniform, have them dress in uniform, set up the room in a similar fashion to the testing room (if it is known), and allot the same amount of time.

Prepare the questions and suggested responses for the mock panelists. Recommend that panelist take good notes on things discussed to provide feedback to the students. Provide a list of the candidates with times and possible information such as where they work for a richer feedback discussion.

Oral Panel Interview

NOTE: Allocate ONE hour for each candidate's mock interview allowing 45 minutes for the interview and 15 minutes for any feedback. Try to have more than one panel if needed based on the number of candidates. Remind candidates they are free to record the interview and the feedback via audio or video. You can also have candidates prepare a resume or work on a written prompt in the class as some examinations may require one or both as a part of the process.

ANNEX D

SAMPLE STUDY WORKSHOP or STUDY PLAN SCHEDULE
WRITTEN AND ORAL PANEL INTERVIEW

*This example can be modified based on which study plan you need: written or oral panel interview preparation. It can also be created for in-person, virtual workshops or study groups.

DATE	TOPIC	MATERIALS NEEDED
Tuesday March 12 5:30 pm start Plan on 2 hours Instructors: Smith and Jones	• Overview of Study Workshop • Scope of Interview/Assessment Center • How to Study Stack • Personnel Evaluations, Education, Application • Leadership Principles, Philosophy • Team Building • Mentoring • Organizational Vision, Values, Strategic Plan, Mission	Identify what study material candidates will need to have available for each study session.

DATE	TOPIC	MATERIALS NEEDED
Tuesday March 19 5:30 pm start Instructors:	• Relational Policing • Community Engagement Strategies • Intelligence Led Policing • Injury & Illness Program • SCIF Management • Employee Welfare • Employee Wellness & Assistance Program	
Tuesday March 26 5:30 pm start Instructors:	• EEO • Laws, Legislative Updates • Ethics • Professionalism • Employee Misconduct/ Investigations • Progressive Discipline • Substance Abuse • Emotional Intelligence • Implicit Bias • Peace Officer Bill of Rights	

Sample Study Plan

DATE	TOPIC	MATERIALS NEEDED
Tuesday April 2 5:30 pm start Instructors:	• Pursuit Policy • Shooting Policy • Incident Command System • Social Unrest/Civil Disturbance • Use of Force • Principled Policing/Procedural Justice • Standard Operating Procedures (SOP)	
Tuesday April 9 5:30 pm start Instructors:	Budget/Fiscal Accountability • Overtime • Scheduling / Resource management • Grants • Civil Liability issues • Workers Compensation • Budget Process & Planning	MIDTERM EXAMS Mini Mock Interviews Scheduled
Tuesday April 16 5:30 pm start Instructors:	• Allied Agency Partnerships • Audits and Inspections (Evidence, Cash, Equipment) • Employee Morale, Motivation, and Inspiration • Labor Relations	

DATE	TOPIC	MATERIALS NEEDED
Tuesday April 23 5:30 pm start Instructors:	• Homeland Security • State Building emergencies • Civil Disturbance, Mutual Aid • Other Items as needed • PRA and release of information	
Tuesday April 30 5:30 pm start Instructors:	Final Review *Create a final study document and outline	
WEEK OF May 1-10	PRACTICE WRITTEN EXAMINATION FORMAL MOCK INTERVIEWS	Panel members and details to be determined. Can be conducted virtually if needed.
Week of May 20-24 July 1	AGENCY INTERVIEWS LIST RELEASE DATE	CONGRATULATIONS, YOU DID IT!

ANNEX E

EXAMPLES OF MOCK INTERVIEW AND SCENARIO QUESTIONS

Equal Employment Opportunity

You are newly promoted and working in an area office, command or agency, when you observe a male and female employee having a heated conversation. As you approach them, both of them walk away. When you later contact the female employee, she begins to cry and share with you that the male employee has been threatening to tell other people in the office about the one date they had. He keeps asking her out and she doesn't want to see him again and has told him so several times. She asks that nothing formal be done but she just wants it to stop. Explain what actions you would take.

Pursuits

You are working a swing shift in a major city when a unit notifies the communication center that they are in pursuit of a black sedan with tinted windows. The unit advises that the initial reason for the contact was that the vehicle matches the description of the suspected vehicle involved in a felony hit and run that occurred earlier in the shift. The pursuit enters the freeway with speeds ranging between 55 and 80 mph in moderate midday traffic. Explain your responsibilities and what actions you would take.

De-escalation, Crisis Intervention and Use of Force

You monitor a call of a pedestrian on the freeway. The communication center advises that the pedestrian is possibly experiencing a mental health crisis. Two of your new officers in separate patrol vehicles arrive on the scene and notify the communications center that the pedestrian is combative and refusing to follow commands. A struggle ensues, and the pedestrian is eventually subdued and placed in handcuffs. As a result of the arrest, the pedestrian sustains significant injuries. Explain what actions you would take.

Survival Guide

Officer Involved Incident and Incident Command System

During a graveyard shift in an urban city while monitoring the radio traffic, you hear an officer broadcast "11-99, shots fired." There are no additional radio transmissions. Upon arriving at the scene, which is in a residential neighborhood, you learn that the suspect has been shot and has succumbed to his injuries. The officer involved in the shooting is physically uninjured and is standing with other officers who have arrived at the scene. Media is beginning to arrive and residents in the community are coming out of their homes. Explain what actions you would take.

Employee Misconduct and Progressive Discipline

You are assigned to the day shift in your local jurisdiction and three months into your new position you need to have a counseling session with a veteran employee with over 20 years of service for failing to take a report on an accident investigation. Additionally, when you review the past performance of the employee, you notice that there have been several informal counseling sessions on this same issue before and on the employee's lack of response to calls for service, beat assistance and availability during the shift. Explain what actions you would take.

Trust and Legitimacy

You are assigned to the day shift in your local city when your commander advises that the community has concerns about recent police actions within your agency and across the country. The media influence has escalated the concerns of prominent community members who are planning a protest at the end of the week. Your commander is concerned about the upcoming protests and feels more should be done to build public trust amongst local community members. Explain how you would address the concerns and what actions you would take.

ANNEX F

EXAMPLE STUDY CHECKLIST FORMAT (EEO)
Equal Employment Opportunity Checklist

Background

☐ **A discrimination complaint is defined as:**

- An allegation of illegal discrimination of which the primary or partial basis of the complaint or cause is the employee's or applicant's race, color, religion, national origin, ancestry, age, sex (includes sexual harassment), physical or mental disability, political affiliation/opinion, marital status, sexual orientation, medical condition, or retaliation.

☐ **Sexual harassment includes:**
- Unwelcome sexual advances, requests for sexual favors, and other verbal or physical conduct of a sexual nature when the conduct explicitly or implicitly affects an individual's employment (quid pro quo), unreasonably interferes with an individual's work performance, or creates an intimidating, hostile, or offensive/hostile work environment.

☐ **Legal Authority:**

- Title VII of the Civil Rights Act of 1964
- California Fair Employment and Housing Act
- Age Discrimination in Employment Act of 1967 (ADEA)
- Americans with Disabilities Act of 1990 (ADA)
- Other related state and federal civil rights laws.

☐ **Action: What action will you take based upon your rank for the examination? Below are a few considerations:**

Resolve at the lowest possible level
- Notify management/commander
- Stop the action; address the issue and bring an immediate end to the inappropriate behavior/practice

- Consult with complainant
- Inform of rights
- Explain the internal and external process
- Inquire as to the desire to file a complaint
- Refer to an EEO counselor
- Inform of freedom from retaliation and to report immediately if it occurs

- Conduct fact finding inquiry
    - Interview witnesses suggested by both parties
    - Review the personnel records of the accused
    - Consult with other supervisors regarding past history and personal observations

- Consult with discriminatory employee
    - Be careful to observe their employee rights
    - Inquire if reported behavior/action occurred
    - Inform the employee that the conduct is unwelcome and must stop
    - Remind the employee of the departmental policy
    - Advise the employee that retaliation is prohibited and may result in an adverse decision
- Document interactions with the complainant and the discriminatory employee

Sexual harassment:

- Take immediate action regarding observed or reported incidents
- Ensure incidents are given serious attention and that timely/appropriate corrective action is taken to remedy the situation

Study Checklist Format

- ☐ Discrimination Complaint: Know the internal complaint process and external complaint process.

- ☐ Prevention: Monitor environment, ongoing training, create a workplace environment free of sexual harassment and discrimination by following policy, address issues promptly and apply appropriate discipline, ensure employees are advised of policy updates, and have access to departmental resources, Employee Assistance Program (EAP) and Peer Support.

- ☐ Paperwork: Training file, complaint log, complaint investigation, closing correspondence.

- ☐ Policy: Ensure all employees are adhering to departmental policy and staying current on annual training.

- ☐ Protected Groups: Know all the protected groups.

- ☐ Examine the potential impacts of violations of EEO rules and regulations to the organizational culture:

  - Loss of internal and external trust
  - Civil Liability
  - Loss of productivity
  - Reduced morale

ANNEX G

ASSESSMENT CENTER OVERVIEW AND APPROACH

An assessment center is used to assess an employee's skills, knowledge, and ability to be suitable and eligible for leadership roles within the organization. Employees will participate in the assessment center process and participate in a series of exercises. The exercises are designed to resemble the job duties and responsibilities and a wide range of competencies to assess the employee's qualifications for the position. Some of the behavioral dimensions for evaluation can include: Leadership, Judgment, Decision Making, Interpersonal Skills, Delegation and other dimensions identified by your organization.

An employee will experience a variety of exercises which will vary depending on the design of the assessment center. The following will cover some of the most common exercises and strategies for better success. For more detailed understanding of assessment centers, you should further research training programs and books to help you prepare.

Potential Assessment Center Exercises

In-Basket

The typical in-basket will contain a series of items of varying importance and priority to simulate daily duties and responsibilities of a manager and above. Consider the multiple activities in the day that include multitasking reports, answering emails, responding to correspondence and dealing with employee matters. The following is a list of possible items that could be included in an in-basket:

- Emails
- Phone messages
- Memos
- Reports
- Internal and external correspondence
- Strategic planning documents

The number of items in the in-box could range from 10-15 or more. Each will have dates, times, names, and content to give you context for what you are handling. The object is to review the information within the in-basket and decide what actions to take for each item.

Most of the contents in the in-basket will have some overlapping correlations to other people, situations, or even have broader implication for the unit, division, or organizational culture and environment.

Things you will want to consider while working through this exercise:

Approach:

- Time management: All exercises of the assessment center process are timed.

- Attention to detail: Make sure to carefully read all instructions; note all of the limitations (resources, dates, times, scheduling conflicts, email or correspondence from and to lines, along with the content and context of the information).

- Read through all items briefly to get a feel for what your full "in-basket" has in it.

- Begin prioritizing and make notes on the documents if needed, or whatever tracking mechanism (calendar, electronic suspense system) that works for you in this type of exercise. Tracking and monitoring mechanisms are often provided so make sure if you use it, which is best, make sure to explain how you will use it. Use any policy, controls, processes and staffing resources available to help facilitate this component.

- Identify what will need to be delegated and to whom and what direction you will give to the person to whom you've delegated the task. Make sure to communicate any documentation, notifications, follow up and how you are planning/coordinating the delegated tasks.

- Include any departmental policy, process, resources, programs, or trending issues that connect to the information.

- Remember, this exercise is designed to evaluate much of the knowledge and abilities on your examination bulletin.

- This is a verbal assessment center. It is imperative that your problem-solving and decision making is done audibly as you work through how you will communicate, assign, notify, analyze, and identify the issue and your solutions. Assessors cannot hear what you are thinking.

- REMEMBER, you may not have time to address all the issues that emerge within the exercise with your resources and/or limitations, or it may not be an immediate priority. Just make sure to acknowledge the issue and explain it to the panel on what you will do and why.

Role-Play

This exercise can be designed to work one-on-one with a subordinate, peer, or someone above you in rank or can involve a group (community, staff, council members). Often you are presenting information either in a meeting, presentation, or even in a counseling session.

Role player roles can also include those who are a part of the group but are not silent actors. Their role may be to create a distraction by being agitated or ask questions which make you lose focus on responding directly to your examination prompt within the time allocations provided. They can also be included to see how you demonstrate some of the dimensions identified in your examination process (i.e., judgment, interpersonal skills, etc.).

Approach:

- Use the preparation time allocated before you are escorted into the room for the actual exercise to practice what you've been studying through your response strategies methods and take notes that will guide your thoughts in the exercise.

- Attention to detail: Make sure to carefully read all of the instructions; note any patterns, concerns, specified information and by whom.

- Consider available resources, dates, times, along with the content and context of information.

- Remember, role playing exercises can be distracting. Be sure to manage your time and work to accomplish your goals that will directly address the examination prompt.

- Personalize your approach and consider the knowledge, abilities, and special characteristics within the examination bulletin.

- When dealing with employee issues, refer to your employee counseling experience. If you haven't had a lot of experience counseling employees, follow these strategies for both the exercise and in reality:
    - Actively listen to the responses from the role player (employee) so you can adjust your approach if needed.
    - Attempt to assess the employee's current workload, work environment and any personal challenges that could be affecting their work performance.
    - Be cognizant of any progressive discipline, development training or employee assistance offered in the past. This will dictate how you may need to escalate disciplinary outcomes, documentation, employee representation, training needs and further resources for assistance.
    - Always be mindful of the employee's rights when in a counseling session or disciplinary processes.
    - While in the counseling session, build a rapport, if possible. Be non-confrontational and genuine by asking how your employee is doing before you move into the purpose of the counseling session.
    - Clarify why you're conducting the meeting which will help to set the tone and context at the outset. Make sure to ask open ended questions to allow for better communication. Doing this should help to give you a better idea of what the underlying issues may be.

- Outline and communicate steps that will work toward resolving the issues. Include the appropriate policy references or expectations and other resources that may be applicable.

- Close the counseling session with clear expectations, disciplinary outcomes, documentation, and when you will be meeting again or following up.

Presentation

The presentation exercises can be a blend of any style of environment: meeting with staff; meeting with your superior; meeting with external stakeholders. External stakeholders could be community groups, city or county council members, media, or other entities with whom your agency has partnerships or that provide a service.

Generally, the exercise will allow you to demonstrate many of the dimensions identified in the examination bulletin which can include leadership, communication, problem solving and interpersonal skills.

Approach:

- Attention to detail: Make sure to carefully read all instructions.

- Use your allocated preparation time to go over your response strategies that you've studied to address the exercise prompt. Make any notes you will need, if allowed, and take them with you as reference to help keep you on track as needed. This is where building an acronym or mind mapping approach in your study habits will reinforce information for easy and organized recall for these exercises. See ANNEX RESOURCES for examples.

- Additionally, you might be offered the opportunity to use visual aids. If so, make sure you have practiced using them ahead of time or they could become a distraction and use too much of your allocated time. If they are required, then definitely practice with them during your study schedule. When using visual aids such as flip charts or "PowerPoint" displays, make sure to keep your information streamlined, concise, organized and try to only highlight points that you plan on speaking in depth about verbally.

- Have an opening, middle and closing to your presentation.

- Be prepared to experience assessor behaviors that may not reflect your enthusiasm or engagement as testing environments are relatively sterile in order to create fairness and consistency with candidates.

- Be in your role, know your authority and/or the process for approval. Do not make promises that you are not able to follow through with due to the chain of command. Inform and educate your audience where possible along with addressing the issue.

Panel Interview in the Assessment Center

The panel interview is designed to further assess your knowledge, abilities and to examine your behavior through your responses within the testing environment. The panel can consist of any mix of assessors to include your agency, community, civil service representatives and other allied agencies. Questions should be derived and correlated by the guidelines within the examination bulletin and created from job descriptions, tasks and duties within your agency policy. Each process is different, so be prepared to respond to several questions within the allocated timeframes given in your instructions. Generally, you will not have much preparation time for this exercise.

Approach:

- In the limited time to prepare, gather your thoughts and think about your response template, strategies, or acronyms you've studied. If allowed, write down your mind map, a process of creating a visual map of information that is organized and correlates to what you've studied that helps with recall.

- You can also create an acronym as a reminder of items to include in your responses. There is an example in Annex L.

- Sometimes you might be allowed to take in notes from the prep time. If you're not sure, ask.

- Attention to detail: read the material that is given to you so you can comprehend and understand what is being asked of you with clarity. You may become stressed and not hear anything a panel member may be saying or even recall the words you read. Pause and verbally express "I'm just going to read this one more time for clarity, thank you." You are in control of your own outcomes, so take control.

- When you complete a question and response, ask to move on to the next question or give clarification so they are not waiting, and you are not losing time. If you are asked a question that you were not overly prepared for, ask to move on to the next one, and then RETURN to that question. In this process, you may begin to regain composure and remember the material that you have studied.

- Using the response strategies that you've practiced will help you navigate even the unexpected question with greater success.

That was a basic overview of an assessment center process and the type of exercises that could be included. I want to additionally share some baseline framework concepts for your response strategies:

Prioritizing

When prioritizing, consider:

- Mitigating Risks: Think about those risks that could be urgent or immediate and the potential risk if not corrected or could continue.

- Required by law/policy: What are the compliance considerations for time frames, and are there any resulting safety concerns? Are there any behavioral situations as a result that involve other personnel, community or third parties? Is the situation ongoing or pervasive? What is the process as defined by policy to address the issue?

- Departmental Importance: It is very important to identify important agency trends and to give them the appropriate priority in your problem-solving considerations. You will want to make sure to accommodate and place them on a higher priority and to ensure that they are handled/addressed and why.

- Command Environment: Consider the affect on employees if these risks are not addressed in a timely manner, or if the situation is delegated to the wrong person. The wrong person is sometimes someone who is actually involved in the issue who may be either a peer, a rank above or higher in the chain of command.

Intervention

Consider any opportunities that:
- Involve safety or an urgent liability issue. This can involve negligent retention of employees as a result of failing to properly supervise or manage out of an incident or to proceed through progressive disciplinary processes as needed.

- If you do not intervene, will the situation continue or get worse?

- Is there a policy, law, or procedure requirement that requires your intervention?

- Will intervening give you more time to find out about the issue/incident that may be sensitive in nature?

- *Example:* Employee needs to take time off and refers to personal problems at home and expresses frustration, sadness, and a sense of hopelessness.

Delegation

Delegation is a good and important tool. It allows you to be an effective and efficient leader as well as providing you an opportunity to develop employees. Things to remember in an assessment center environment:

- Knowing when to delegate work and to whom and making sure to select the appropriate rank/classification of employee to perform that work. It is important to know if the work you are about to delegate is something that are you required to do as opposed to someone else doing it and will there be any negative outcomes if you don't handle it personally.

- Due dates, timelines.

- Ensuring that the work is done according to proper procedures and is completed in a timely manner.

- Having appropriate follow up and monitoring procedures in place.

Planning and Coordinating

Planning and coordinating involve a myriad of activities. What you want to consider:

- Staffing resource allocations and needs. For example, shifts, working with allied partners and identifying evolving situations and adjusting.

- Budget planning for the short-term and the long-term.

- Protests and large-scale events planned or unplanned. Personnel, equipment, and logistics.

- Think about the methodology for how things will be accomplished and by whom.

- Personnel misconduct investigations or departmental program management.

- Balancing administrative situations and field incidents in coordinating and planning. For example:

    In an in-basket exercise – after identifying a problem with your subordinates working through a conflict resolution issue, you could include how you will handle the immediate problem and include more planning and coordinating through your follow up of weekly meetings with both of the parties involved and to create channels of ongoing communication.

    Presentation exercise: ICS with unified command working with allied agencies on a critical incident. Include the immediate planning/coordinating and the additional planning/coordinating through training, after action plans and other integrated meetings.

ANNEX H

ORAL PANEL INTERVIEW AND ASSESSMENT CENTER RESPONSE STRATEGY TECHNIQUES

Preparation for an oral panel interview/assessment center response is having a plan with strategies and mental thought mapping exercises that will ensure that you will be efficient, focused, and effective. These are a few examples of how to build a plan for navigating your responses and can be adapted to your own style for more authenticity.

When considering how to approach response strategies keep a baseline around the following:

- PRE-INCIDENT, INCIDENT AND POST INCIDENT (PIP).
- PREVENTIVE, MITIGATING, OR DISPOSITION (PMD). *INCIDENT/ISSUE/SCENARIO

STEP 1: Consider some of the elements or at least the most important elements that you will want to be able to identify in any questions, situations, or scenarios.

Here is a baseline rule of thumb for elements to consider:

Policy: Any policy related to the scenario, specific and/or peripheral. Include any other organizational overlaps and connectivity to other disciplines or laws. Resources, references, technology, and other tools provided through policy.

Law: Are there any compliance, regulatory, authority or legislative laws pertaining to this issue? If so, identify those laws and be comfortable understanding and referencing them in your response versus just citing the section of law. Be thorough.

Training: Everything has a training component. Evaluate all training possibilities that are preventative, ongoing, and that can be applied as a learning reinforcement or part of employee development.

Liability: As you move up in rank, you must always be assessing risk. Make sure to consider the larger trending industry case laws and litigation cases facing all agencies. Try to look beyond the incident to identify the root cause which could include negligent issues regarding the employee relative to his/her supervision/management, training deficiencies or processes, as well as ineffective behavior modification alternatives. When identifying risk, also look for resolutions that will minimize cost to the organization financially and mitigate the loss of trust from the public or other stakeholders.

Discipline vs Development (or both): It is of the utmost importance to have a good understanding of the complexity of progressive discipline, bargaining unions, police associations, and employee misconduct investigatory processes. Make sure to respect the employee's rights and to treat the employee properly throughout the process. Know the difference between interim reporting and any other employee development training options.

Be sure to properly gauge an employee's discipline with the egregiousness of his or her conduct. It will either be clear that there are no suitable developmental options, leaving only disciplinary ones to be implemented. However, there are many times that there is room for both.

Know what resources are available to the employee through the Employee Assistance Program and the representation they are entitled to during the process.

Follow up/Controls: With any scenario or oral interview question, you will need to consider what subsequent or after actions are needed in order to complete the process. Consider what is needed from the actual incident (i.e. documentation, notifications and after actions). You should then consider the employee, any aggrieved parties or complainants, victims, witnesses, other employees, and the organization. Was there an impact on the community? Was the media involved initially and is some follow up now needed? Will any additional training or further monitoring be needed?

Notifications: Notifications are separate from follow up and control because organization has specific guidelines for proper notification procedures. There are notification procedures for daily incidents as well as clearly defined criteria for large scale incidents that are common sense. Most notification protocols are designed to keep those above you in the chain of command informed.

Make sure to note the importance of trending politically sensitive issues and other peripheral incidents involving other agencies that will have residual impacts on all agencies. To give some perspective, KNOW your policy and think who, what, why, when and where will your notifications be seen both internally and externally.

Community Impacts (internal/external): With the rise of impactful events over the last several years, it's important to monitor and identify lingering effects both internal and external to the agency especially after any large scale significant incidents that occur either locally, nationally or globally. Internally, assess your teams and create access through communication, transparency and engaged leadership. Allow them opportunities to share their concerns and offer them resources if needed.

Externally, there will be components to address involving community, media, allied agency partners, and other stakeholders. Consider a similar approach by creating engaged relational policing strategies and building in considerations for proactive and reactive responses depending on the scenario or question.

STEP 2: Developing Appropriate Response Strategies

Here are some baseline considerations for developing strategies and techniques for responses:

Know Your Role/Position: Always look at the incident from the lens of the position you are seeking and above. Expand your own understanding of both the technical and broader implications. As you rise in rank, you are expected to be able to do both and so much more. Know what authority you have in your rank and within your organization when involved in various situations. Do you need approval, or is there a process outside of your role?

Identify issues/topics/trends: What issues/topics/trends are important to the organization, governing councils, community, labor unions, the law enforcement and public safety profession nationally? Seek information from your chain of command and/or research organizations such as International Association of Chiefs of Police (IACP), Police Executive Research Forum (PERF), National Organization of Black Law Enforcement Executives (NOBLE), U.S. Department of Justice, Community Oriented Policing Services (US DOJ COPS) and American Society for Evidence Based Policing (ASEBP).

These are just a few of the resources available but do your research and understand the implications of issues on the broader landscape that impact your agency.

Identify Technology and other resources you will need: There are many technological tools such as software programs for analytics, platforms for social media, databases for employee training and investigations, suspense files and early intervention systems available. Some examples of policing technology include facial recognition software, automated license plate readers, gunshot detection systems, drones, Body-Worn Cameras (BWC), and Mobile Video Audio Recording Systems (MVARS).

Remember all of the technology resources that are identified in policy that can assist you in your role to complete tasks, assess data, and complete required reporting. Also include your understanding and knowledge of which electronic forms are required for documentation and timeframes.

STEP 3: Develop response strategies and techniques that will be inclusive of all considerations. In addition, most examination processes require you to manage time, provide responses for complex questions or scenarios while managing your stress.

Have a systematic approach and use it. It will help reduce stress and better manage time.

STEP 4: An extra consideration if you have a question involving elements of a scenario/question where elements of project management could enhance your response:

Basic project management could include personnel investigations, citizen complaints, planning for events, actual organizational program management, etc. Always lead with policy and the process outlined therein and if needed, build in some elements of the following:

- Identify team/stakeholders
- Define goals
- Define roles and responsibilities
- Assign duties/roles/assignments
- Set timelines and priorities for deliverables
- Create a suspense system/project tracking mechanism
- Ensure ongoing effective communication
- Re-evaluate milestones
- Work with your management team on updating status and readjusting priorities as needed.

These activities within an exercise help demonstrate problem solving capabilities, knowledge of departmental processes, policy, and leadership. Additionally, it can demonstrate the ability to communicate effectively; organize, analyze, and develop solutions through teamwork.

ANNEX I

SAMPLE PROMPTS

ORAL PANEL INTERVIEW QUESTIONS AND

WRITTEN EXERCISES

- To ensure the health and safety of employees before, during and after an incident, what actions would you take to handle both the incident command system (ICS) for scene management and the human side of the incident for employees.

- Describe a significant leadership challenge you faced where you learned an important lesson. Explain the challenge and give examples of the lessons learned.

- How have you effectively managed limited resources to meet competing demands and organizational goals? How has this experience prepared you for your role in this position?

- To build better trust and legitimacy internally and externally, please tell us how you will implement this philosophy and its strategies.

- In your role, please describe what steps you would take to build better relational policing through community engagement strategies.

- The Equal Employment Opportunity Agency (EEO) has developed and delivered a set of guidelines for creating a workplace environment free from sexual harassment and discrimination. What is your role in the EEO process and within the organization?

- Allied partnerships are critical to meeting the mission of the organization. Describe when you have had to collaborate, coordinate, or oversee an incident or program involving other allied partners. Explain your role, what was accomplished and what did you learn.

- Please describe how your prior work history has prepared you to work in an environment with a firmly established chain of command.

- Please describe how your education, training, and/or experience have prepared you to handle multiple projects with competing deadlines.

- Explain and describe an experience where you had to analyze information and how you came up with the best solution to the problem.

- Describe a time you had to deal with a difficult employee and how you handled the situation.

- Describe your knowledge of departmental policy on use of force situations and share an example when you had to control, detain or use force on an offender.

- Explain your leadership style.

- Describe how you prioritize, organize and manage teams on a project.

ANNEX J

PRACTICE EXERCISE ~ CAPTAIN

Panel Interview/Presentation/Assessment Center
(Can be modified for any classification or rank)

You are a new commander and have been given direction from your sector chief to attend a meeting this afternoon with the local board of supervisors. The sector chief briefly shared concerns regarding several significant fatal collisions in the county jurisdiction of your command involving members of the community. What actions will you take?

EXAMPLE OF THINGS TO CONSIDER FOR RESPONSE PREPARATION AND ASSESSMENT OF THE ISSUE WHEN ADDRESSING THIS SCENARIO:

- Acknowledgement of the timeframe for the meeting and audience of the meeting.

- Resources identified to assist with the meeting (reports, data, statistics).

- Identify any personnel (if needed) that might accompany you to the meeting.

- Familiarize yourself with the individuals on the board if possible (online).

- Review past engagement reports to be aware of last contact and what was addressed (know the policy and your role in it).

- Review details of the collision if available and prepare to share what is releasable (PRA) Public Records Act/(What's in the media already?), AND IF NOT, be able to explain the process for collision investigations in order to create transparency.

- Consideration for working closely with the family of those involved to keep them updated in the investigation.

- Share the departmental/area approach to addressing: Enforcement, Education, and Engineering. Include your plan to address any immediate concerns.

- Discuss active listening to hear their concerns.

- Identify and discuss any additional measures for re-visiting with the board, or within the command.

- Notifications that are needed both internally and externally. What other stakeholders should be involved (County or city, other allied law enforcement)?

- Internal considerations for reviewing activity and performance of personnel and supervisor/manager engagement issues.

- Discussion with managers, supervisors and officers regarding the meeting. Share expectations and be open to innovative strategies from staff.

- Reminder about professionalism, service delivery, mission, and values.

- Correlate to the Strategic Plan and other organizational and/or city initiatives, where possible.

ANNEX K

SAMPLE IN-BASKET

PRACTICE EXERCISE

(Captain and above but can be modified for any classification or rank)

Review: Important items (criticality) vs urgent items (time constraints).

Look for connectivity between items and a bigger understanding of command challenges in addition to those associated with individual items.

Prioritize: Handle the important and urgent items first; justify and explain decision making for all items.

Justify Approach/Decisions: Engage the panel with verbal communication through problem solving and what, why, when and how you will manage the in-basket. Thinking out loud shows your ability at problem-solving. Be strategic and audible.

Identify Resources/Options/Alternatives: Determine who should and could handle personnel resource needs for issues both internally and externally. Include commander resources/references. Don't forget how to leverage technology, if possible.

Follow Up: Monitor and track who can follow up if you cannot with any planning or coordinating as to time frames. Be sure to include policy and processes.

Make Notifications: Internal and external; within the command, division, agency, community, individually, collectively; before, during, after; who needs to be notified for immediate response, awareness notifications or to be involved in the incident/issue.

SCENARIO:

You are a new commander stopping by the office today (December 23) only to drop off your equipment and pick up your departmental command cell phone before catching a flight for your prepaid vacation. Your initial start date is not for another two weeks (January 7).

When you arrive, you notice your sector chief has sent several emails with issues for you to address before leaving for vacation out of the country. There are other additional items in your in-basket requiring your attention as well.

Your sector chief is no longer available by phone until (January 8).

Your staffing is limited in the office as several of your supervisors are on vacation and unavailable. The shift is being overseen by an "officer in charge." The one lieutenant in your command has retired. The position has been vacant for two months and one of your sergeants has been filling in as an acting lieutenant. The acting lieutenant is unavailable due to a recent surgery.

Additionally, you have to leave in exactly one hour to catch your flight for your cruise (no cell service).

Once you leave on vacation no one will be able to contact you for a week until you return (January 1). You will not have an opportunity to follow up on anything until you return and no ability to clarify information in your absence.

You will be completely out of contact with anyone while on vacation until you return January 1.

You should take any action to set up activities for your return prior to leaving the office, even if such activities are not specific in-basket items.

ITEM #1

Date: December 13

To: Acting Lieutenant

From: Board of Supervisors, District 3

Subject: Request for meeting the Board of Supervisors is requesting a meeting to discuss departmental traffic safety responsibilities and emergency incident planning. Follow up with our administrative secretary NLT than December 23 regarding further details. The scheduled presentation is for January 7.

ITEM #2

Date: December 23

To: New Commander

From: Sector Chief

Subject: Request for Information

Headquarters has requested your command provide statistical information on enforcement contacts from June through December. The information is requested to include: location of stop; time of day; violation; and race.

This information is due to HQ NLT January 5.

ITEM #3

Date: December 23

To: New Commander

From: Sector Chief

Subject: Complaint

I received a call from the senator's office requesting a complaint to be filed against one of your supervisors for rude and discourteous conduct. The initial conversation with the complainant was taken by me personally and i will need you to assign the complaint. We can discuss further when i return from vacation.

ITEM #4

Date: December 22

To: New Commander

From: Clerical Supervisor

Subject: Personal

I hope you will keep this confidential. I have been having problems at home and the Acting Lieutenant does not understand. The way I am treated at work has made me very stressed. I know my work performance is slacking but I have a lot going on. I'm only letting you know because the Acting Lieutenant raised their voice at me in front of other staff today and it made me feel humiliated. I wanted my side of what happened to be shared versus just the Acting Lieutenant.

I hope you can find time to meet with me when you report to the office. I am going on vacation December 23-January 5.

ITEM #5

Date: December 22

To: New Commander

From: Clerical Supervisor

Subject: Annual Evaluations

Commander, Annual Evaluations for several of my clerical staff are due January 5. I submitted them to the acting lieutenant two weeks ago and have not received them back. Please advise me on the status of the reports.

Other Exercise Suggestions:
Number of items in an in-basket will vary between 5 and 15 items. To increase your preparation and practice include miscellaneous reports/ statistics/forms you would find in your in-basket to build out more items for this exercise.

ANNEX L

MNEMONICS (ACRONYMS) BUILDING EXERCISE

ACRONYM BUILDING: Mnemonic devices are strategies, and a system, a person can use to help improve their ability to remember something. The process allows for a shorter way to associate data or other information you need to remember with a word, sentence, or image.

Developing an acronym to create response development should be modified to your style and comfort. Try to correlate what you are learning to something you have experienced. Cultivate an active interest in the information and the connectivity will resonate more with you. Below are samples of acronym building.

ACRRID PIP
- Assess Alternatives
- Communication
- Resolution Strategies
- Risk assessment
- Identify the Issue
- Documentation
- Pre-Incident
- Incident
- Post Incident

Create your own with these headings, or from those above, to build Acronym(s):

- Global
- Problem Analysis
- Considerations
- Solutions
- Training
- Notification/Inform
- Follow up/Controls
- Documentation
- Best Practices
- Trend assessment

To further reinforce your understanding, practice taking one of the sample issues below, or choose your own, and practice creating an acronym you are comfortable with and then address the issue. Allow yourself only 5 minutes and then repeat.

Sample Issue: Mutual Aid, Employee Performance, Use of Force, Emergency Incident Planning, Budget Process & Planning, Training, Recruitment, Community Engagement, Team Building, Workforce Planning.

ANNEX M

BASIC PROJECT MANAGEMENT STRATEGIES

PROJECT MANAGEMENT (basic) may be required in some response strategies to demonstrate knowledge and ability for time management, team building, efficiency, and meeting expectations.

The following is an example of some elements of project management to follow on any project which could include public safety issue planning projects, response to after action reporting, internal investigations, or response to citizen complaints on community issues the agency is coordinating, etc.

- Identify team/stakeholders
- Define goals
- Brainstorm objectives and obstacles
- Define roles and responsibilities
- Assign duties/roles/assignments
- Set timelines and priorities for deliverables and who to
- Create a suspense system/project tracking mechanism
- Ongoing effective communication
- Re-evaluate milestones
- Work with your management on updating status and readjusting priorities if needed

Note: Reminder, any system you develop to help you retain information and create organized responses will help demonstrate:

- Problem solving capabilities
- Knowledge of departmental processes and policy
- Leadership
- Ability to communicate effectively, organize, and use critical thinking
- Develop solutions through teamwork and delegation

ANNEX N

MENTAL THOUGHT MAPPING EXERCISE

Mental Thought Mapping: A way to chart out your thoughts and ideas that can help organize information visually. Usually, you will start with a main idea or topic and then create branches of connected or correlated information. From the initial ideas, you can create more connections and ideas until you've gone through your streams of thought. After you've exhausted your mental thought mapping, you can begin to narrow down and streamline your main points. The visual exercise will help you retain the information. This exercise helps you to increase your verbal and written communication and ability to demonstrate broader knowledge on those ideas or topics.

In this exercise, practice thought leadership through writing out as much information as you can in 5 minutes. Create supporting ideas and expand out within each branch until your time is completed. After the exercise, try it again.

Issue: Mutual Aid, Employee Performance, Emergency Incident Planning, Budget, Overtime, Recruitment, Community Engagement. (FACILITATOR WILL PROVIDE THE PROMPT ISSUE FOR THE EXERCISE).

DEDICATION

This book is dedicated to the professionals in public safety and law enforcement industries who are seeking a desire to promote within their organization and answer the call to higher leadership. I hope the guide allows room for thoughtful consideration of the promotional and leadership journey to better prepare the pathway. Many will travel the road toward upward mobility; however, only a few will understand the gravity and responsibility of the required leadership that must accompany it.

Please share this guide with those you feel would benefit from deepening their foundational assessment of the readiness to promote and need the framework for how to prepare for it.

Feel free to contact me at *jonniredick@jlconsultingsolutions.com* with any questions, suggestions, or discussion.

Please take time to post a review on Amazon.com or find me on my website at *www.jlconsultingsolutions.com.*

You can also follow me on Instagram @jonniredick or find me on LinkedIn at *https://www.linkedin.com/in/jonniredick/.*

ABOUT THE AUTHOR

Retired Assistant Chief Jonni Redick was with the California Highway Patrol (CHP) for 29 years. The CHP is an organization with over 11,000 employees of which over 7,000 are sworn officers. She held the position of Assistant Chief in the Golden Gate Division of the CHP, which covers all nine Bay Area counties including the San Francisco California area. In this position, she assisted with the accountability and oversight of 16 field commands with over 1,600 personnel and over 7 million in population.

She retired in December, 2017 out of the Valley Division in the Sacramento region where she oversaw eight CHP commands. This division included the 3rd largest communications center in the state which handles over one million 911 calls annually. She had been the incident commander for multiple critical incidents, civil disturbances, mutual aid events, and other high-profile tactical occurrences.

Over her career, she worked throughout California including the Ontario, Ventura, Hayward, Stockton, San Jose, and Contra Costa CHP offices, and has held all ranks. She was the first female captain of the Contra Costa CHP Area in Martinez, CA where she worked with 18 allied agencies to collectively provide service to an 802 square-mile region.

Her training and instructional background includes many areas of expertise: leadership and promotional development, cultural diversity, procedural justice, implicit bias, and leadership coursework. For over a decade, she instructed first line supervisors, middle managers, and command training within her organization.

She is a certified California State Personnel Board Chairperson and has participated both as a chairperson and agency representative on promotional examination oral interview panels and in examination development.

In addition, she is the CEO of JL Consulting Solutions, LLC, where she is committed to enhancing the public safety and law enforcement industry to effectively serve the complexities of crime issues, community engagement and create a culture of ethical leadership. In an evolving public safety climate, she works to cultivate relationships that will strengthen the trust quotient of leadership by identifying intrinsic intangibles within leadership paradigms. Through her coaching, she endeavors to develop a dynamic set of skills and strategies essential for modern law enforcement professionals and organizations.

She is a member of the National Organization of Black Law Enforcement Executives (NOBLE), the American Association of University of Women (AAUW), the National Black MBA Association (NBMBAA), and the International Association of Chiefs of Police (IACP).

Retired Chief Redick is a graduate of the California Peace Officer Standard and Training (POST) Command College with course work in Enhanced Leadership; Futures Forecasting and Economic Issues; Politics of Change, and Technological and Environmental Issues. She holds a Master of Science degree in Law Enforcement and Public Safety Leadership (LEPSL) from the University of San Diego. She is also an adjunct faculty member for a local community college instructing the next generation of law enforcement and for a private university in California instructing executive leaders in law enforcement and public safety leadership from across the country.

Additionally, she is a public speaker and author of *Black, White & Blue: Surviving the Sifting.*

J.L.R.
Jonni Redick

Retired Assistant Chief,
California Highway Patrol

Author • Consultant • Leader

Web www.jonniredick.com

Mail jonniredick@jlconsultingsolutions.com

Social www.linkedin.com/in/jonniredick

Welcome to the Curry family. Got an idea for a book? Contact Curry Brothers Marketing and Publishing Group, LLC. We are not satisfied until your publishing dreams come true. We specialize in all genres of books, especially religion, leadership, family history, poetry, and children's literature. There is an African Proverb that confirms, *"When an elder dies, a library closes."* We advise, be careful who tells your family history. Are their values your family's values? Our staff will navigate you through the entire publishing process, and we take pride in going the extra mile by exceeding your publishing goals.

Improving the world one book at a time!

Curry Brothers Publishing, LLC
PO Box 247
Haymarket, VA 20168
(719) 466-7518 & (615) 347-9124
Visit us at *www.currybrotherspublishing.com*

www.ingramcontent.com/pod-product-compliance
Lightning Source LLC
Chambersburg PA
CBHW040420100526
44589CB00021B/2774